Awaken Your Multidimensional Soul

CONVERSATIONS
WITH THE

Z's

BOOK TWO

ALSO BY LEE HARRIS

Energy Speaks:
Messages from Spirit on Living, Loving, and Awakening

Conversations with the Z's, Book One:
The Energetics of the New Human Soul

Awaken Your Multidimensional Soul

CONVERSATIONS
WITH THE

Z's

BOOK TWO

LEE HARRIS
with DIANNA EDWARDS

New World Library
Novato, California

New World Library
14 Pamaron Way
Novato, California 94949

Text design by Tona Pearce Myers

Library of Congress Cataloging-in-Publication data is available.

First printing, May 2023
ISBN 978-1-60868-856-2
Ebook ISBN 978-1-60868-857-9
Printed in Canada on 100% postconsumer-waste recycled paper

New World Library is proud to be a Gold Certified Environmentally Responsible Publisher. Publisher certification awarded by Green Press Initiative.

10   9   8   7   6   5   4   3   2   1

CONTENTS

A NOTE FROM LEE

You are all existing in the past, the present, and the future
simultaneously....As much as you can, enjoy the experience
of being alive now. Tell people what you feel you need
to tell them. Show them what you need to show them.
Live in a way that lights you up as much as possible.

— THE Z'S

Welcome to Book Two and the continuation of a very exciting and unique journey.

Conversations with the Z's is a series of dialogues with the group of eighty-eight ninth-dimensional beings that I've been channeling since they first spoke to me in 1999. The conversations are facilitated by my good friend, psychotherapist Dianna Edwards.

You can find more background on the origins of the series in *Conversations with the Z's, Book One: The Energetics of the New Human Soul.* Suffice it to say, once these conversations got rolling, it was clear that the Z's had an awful lot to share, and Dianna was the perfect partner to ask them just the right questions.

The quote on the previous page is a small sample of the life-affirming insights the Z's share in these pages. The purpose of this work is to allow us to move energy and expand ourselves — to awaken the multidimensional soul within each of us. To this end, Dianna and the Z's cover a vast range of spiritual territory, offering guidance on how we can navigate the "unnerving times," as the Z's put it, that we find ourselves in at this moment on planet Earth.

The conversations in this book touch on subjects including humanity's evolution toward higher vibrations; our connection with guides and angels and how to strengthen it; the nature of premonitions, intuition, and psychic messages; exit points; the reshaping of the Universe that is currently underway; and so much more.

The Z's also offer heaps of practical advice, such as how to free yourself from self-judgment; how to shed imprints of trauma and persecution from past lives; how to navigate the comparison energy inherent in social media; and how to amplify your heart energy, which they call "the most important, abundant, and creational energy on Earth."

Of course, these profound subjects can bring up a lot of reactions in us. I know from my many years of leading courses, live workshops, and numerous group online events that our nervous systems often require gentle calibration to process new information, especially when such information has the potential to challenge our existing belief systems. If we can give ourselves the time and space to digest the information and integrate it, then our chance for growth, including those wonderful quantum leaps, expands exponentially. These conversations offer the opportunity to do all of this and more, if you, the reader, want them to.

I always want to honor that the choice of what you take away from any of the work the Z's and I have brought forth is just that, *your* choice. Take your time as you read these conversations. Take the words in, sit with them, and ask, "How does this information feel in my body?"

If at any point it feels challenging or scary, then I recommend taking a break from the material and, better yet, making a note of the part that challenged you. You could mark that place in the book and also ask yourself: "What arose in me in response to the information — what thoughts, feelings, or triggers?" Jot down a few things, and then reflect on what came to you.

Sometimes it is the very act of *noticing* ourselves that sparks the breakthrough moment we need. When we begin to notice that a certain topic or subject consistently generates fear or defensiveness in us, we can start to investigate the origin of our fear and see if it is still valid for us. We can ask ourselves:

- Where did this fear come from?
- Is it an inherited belief I am carrying, or is there a past history or trauma that is getting triggered?

- When did I first notice this reaction in myself?
- What do I need to do to let go and support myself through this?

Asking these kinds of questions can begin to gently shift our awareness, help us see beyond limiting patterns, and send us on a healing journey that can lead to better and more expanded lives.

One of the most fascinating realities to me is how our personal healing journeys take place in stages and layers. Like peeling an onion, we keep getting deeper, closer to the heart of ourselves and our heart consciousness, as we move through life.

Likewise, the Z's have often explained that each time you listen to or read their words, you will hear them differently, as they will work on different layers of you.

I have certainly experienced this to be true, and I have seen and heard audience members experience this phenomenon too. A participant will be absolutely sure that the Z's said something they didn't, because of what the participant was needing (or choosing) to hear. When I have pointed that out, the person has revisited the material and, to their surprise, heard it completely differently. I have had the exact same experience myself with the Z's' words.

So, if you are loving and enjoying the conversations in the book, please read as much as you like as often as you wish. But if, for you, the material is a lot to digest or is a bit triggering, reading in smaller sections and then taking a break can be the perfect way to absorb it. As can rereading any sections that may initially give you pause or stir up unexpected feelings and thoughts.

Dianna and I have gratefully received some wonderful testimonials for these conversations. For example, in the words of Deva Premal (whose beautiful and uplifting music with Miten plays regularly in my house):

> *I just opened the book to a random page, and the message I got was exactly the answer to a question I have been carrying. We usually can't take the cosmic answers to our human questions fully in, but once in a while, the answer goes straight in and transforms us forever. This book has the power to do just that.*

I am with Deva here. A great and alternative way to use this book (or any book of a similar frequency) is exactly as she has described: just open to a random page, and see what appears to you.

The Z's, Dianna, and I all know that Book One and Book Two are the very important "overture" (to quote the Z's) to the rest of the series. At the time of this release of Book Two, we are already beginning the recordings for Book Five. While the audio recordings of the conversations we have with the Z's are released to my members' community, The Portal, faster than the print version can become available, Dianna and I trust that the information they are giving us is perfectly timed with what the greater world will be ready to hear when the books are ultimately released.

I recently shared with a friend that even though my energy is of course a part of these books, they don't feel like "my" books. They are instead what I would term "a collaboration of oneness." What do I mean by that? The books are Dianna and the Z's' connection to you, the audience, in the present and future; and they're a collaboration of Dianna's own personal stories and professional experiences, as well as the Z's' wisdom and my energy supporting it all. And then, of course, they're a collaboration with the publishing team of New World Library and my team at Lee Harris Energy Productions.

I know Dianna spends an enormous amount of time feeling and connecting with what she believes the collective energy would benefit from knowing. In fact, she has already sketched out a long-term vision of the next six books. However, she is willing to and delightfully capable of adjusting quickly to rearrange the content midconversation to suit the needs of the timelines that seem to be in such flux at this time. She has done this quite a few times already in the flow of the conversations.

I say "delightfully" because Dianna has learned the power of having a sense of humor about life. Instead of falling into despair over an unexpected turn, Dianna always finds the lighter side, the humor, so she can raise the conversation to a higher vibration and carry on. I admire her process, and what is uplifting to me is that she says it is this very same trait in me that keeps her enjoying the journey of these books. Let's be honest — where would any of us be without a sense of humor about it all?!

So yes, there is a history to our friendship and the work of the books, and there is a destiny throughline. But the Z's make it clear that Dianna and I have free will over how many of these books we will do together. The Z's address that and more in the final conversation in this book, which Dianna, with a big smile on her face, calls "Behind the Scenes with the Z's."

I hope you enjoy this journey.

With love,
Lee Harris
December 2022

ABOUT THE
CONVERSATIONS

These conversations between Dianna and the Z's took place privately in November 2021 and April 2022 and were recorded in audio form.

The text for this book has been edited to help it flow better for the reader.

Certain passages from the Z's that are of particular importance are italicized in a larger font so they will stand out. If you, the reader, wish to simply "dip in" to the book, you can skim through and read those passages to get little doses of insight.

This book contains conversations four through eight, while conversations one through three are in *Conversations with the Z's, Book One: The Energetics of the New Human Soul.*

Chapter One

CONVERSATION FOUR

Topics

- What it means to be human
- More light is coming to Earth than ever before
- The power of words
- Admiration and separation
- Allowing yourself to feel well-being
- Traditional archetypes changing

CONVERSATION FOUR

DIANNA:

Welcome back to *Conversations with the Z's*. This is conversation four. Welcome, Z's.

THE Z'S:

Good. Welcome. It's a pleasure to be in the conversation loop and flow once more, and it's also beneficial for all who are reading this to be in a conversation loop within themselves. For these conversations that we are having with you are also inspiring and opening conversations that the readers are having with themselves and their own souls. That is how the frequency exchange works.

DIANNA:

Thank you for explaining that. I want to move into talking about what it means to be human. In your recording "The New Human Soul," you say you prefer to call the third dimension "the planetary grid that grounds and anchors humanity as humanity." Are there other planets that have planetary grids that anchor their humanity?

THE Z'S:

Yes, although humanity is not of origin on other planets at this time. There have been other planets that have had life, but they no longer have life, and it is intended that in the years to come, there will be planets that will be introducing life. It all very much depends on what plays out in the next three to five hundred years on the Earth. For humanity is going through its own shift, which will, in turn, alter the grid that humanity has been, shall we say, placed into. It is gravity. It holds you here in human form. It also keeps the species alive.

The question now for the evolution of humankind is, What will the new human soul become, and how will that frequency-shift change the levels of consciousness on the planet? So, the consciousness on Earth is rising in tandem with the levels of consciousness in the Universe. The reason that the human is elevating at this time is because of that rising level of consciousness. However, humans are strong transmitters.

What is yet to be seen is what will happen when the particular grouping of humans who are incarnate on the planet at this time transmit higher frequencies. This will be especially more evident ten to fifty years from now. What is the frequency effect of more awakened humans on not only the planet but also the energetic grid that humans have for so long been a part of, and feeding, and cocreating? Yes, the energetic grid is what keeps you all, shall we say, in place. But you are all incarnate at a time when it was always expected that the grid would start to open and lose density.

DIANNA:

I understand the gravity keeping us here. How else does the grid keep us alive?

THE Z'S:

You could look at the grid that humans are in energetically as analogous to oxygen. So, in much the same way that humans need oxygen to survive (the current physical form of the human anyway), you could say that the grid is the oxygen through which you all get to breathe. In that sense, the grid is serving you rather than holding you. We understand that you will need to see the grid in different ways, at different times when you are considering it.

But the other aspect of the grid that must be spoken of is, some several thousand years ago, the grid was, shall we say, weighed down in a way that did not allow higher-consciousness energies to continue to flourish. This was done by a group not from Earth who arrived on Earth and decided to weigh the grid down in order to (this is a word we have to be careful of, but it is the only word we can give you) enslave humanity. We know that sounds dramatic, and that can scare some of you, but what we mean by the use of that word is that the group wanted to keep humanity pinned down and not allow humans to reach their potential.

This was part of what you would call "galactic war." This kind of warfare takes place all the time. Earth has an obsession with war, but it was not born on Earth. The war energy template was brought to Earth and was used to, shall we say, embed certain lower frequencies in humans and to disconnect humanity from being in touch with the spirit of the Earth. For (we have alluded to this in different ways over the years) one of the most powerful forces on your Earth cannot be seen. That is not because it is in the realm of spirit. It is because it is buried deep within the Earth herself.

DIANNA:

Can you speak to what that is?

THE Z'S:

Yes and no. We can give you pieces, but we are not at liberty to disclose the whole picture, not because we are being deceptive or in any way trying to withhold things from you. There are certain universal laws at work that allow us to give pieces at a time that will allow you to build your path at the right pace. Too much too soon could disrupt, destabilize, or blow up the consciousness momentum that is currently building in a very good way on Earth. As a people, you are beginning to birth freedom consciousness, even though we are aware that right now many of you are dealing with the opposite of that: something that does not look like freedom consciousness at all.

Much of *that* agenda (the idea behind further entrapping humans) comes from the same source of energy that several thousand years ago wanted to make the grid denser than it was supposed to be. We will describe it this way: Inside the Earth there are both actual crystals and energetic crystals that are now emanating vibrationally. Many of these have "come online" in just the last few decades, which is a very short period of time. But what they are doing is heating up the Earth from inside, heating up the frequencies.

These crystals are actually beginning to burn through and dissolve much of the grid density that was enforced upon your planet several thousand years ago. You are going to see the next couple of decades as a time of tumultuousness, chaos, and unpredictability because what you are actually burning through is a period of your history that was, shall we say, tampered with. You were given an energy template that impeded human growth and stopped humans from interacting with the elemental and energetic forces that exist within your planet.

So, although many of you think of looking up to the sky for your spiritual energy, we would ask you also to look down. For the Earth is full of both actual crystals and energetic crystals. Meaning, crystals can travel. They emit. For example, inside the Earth, you have certain key crystals that have been positioned there for millennia, and they were always designed to be a part of the evolution of not only humankind but the Earth herself and what she is doing universally.

We'll put it this way: any being on another planet right now looking across at Earth would not be very aware of humanity. Now, they may be vaguely aware of humanity, but what they would experience is the Earth herself. While you are all contributing to the energy of Earth right now, what they would mostly be aware of is what she is emitting and what she is pulsing out. The Earth has a pulse, and that pulse is readable and also audible for many. The pulse is quickening inside the Earth. So, these energetic crystals that we referred to a moment ago form when the energy from an actual crystal transposes itself, creating an auric field around itself. And when that auric field merges with the auric field of other crystals, new crystalline energy can be born.

You humans tend to think of crystals as something you can hold in your hand or see in form. But the energetic crystals we're referring to are created when the auras of those physical crystals connect with other crystals and create new auric crystalline fields. The auric crystalline grid in the Earth is itself speeding up at this time, and so more of you are being, we will say, hit by those energies.

Many of you often look to the sky or what is going on electrically, electromagnetically. And one of the reasons that we often say, "Sit on the ground or get on the ground when you are feeling overwhelmed," is because what many of you are tuning in to are the light and sound waves that are coming from inside the Earth, moving through your body, and creating a frisson of energy. When you sit down on the Earth, you are willing to contact that energy. You are willing to combine with it. So, you are no longer in the, shall we say, "wobbliness" of it all. You are able to connect with and collide with the crystalline energy under the ground.

There are many different beings living in your Earth, most of them elemental. You cannot see these with the human eye, but they are very busy at work at this time. And so, what you are actually seeing humans play out on the surface of the planet are the final energy templates of war, control, and manipulation.

We know that many of you may find the above statement difficult and that the energies of war, control, and manipulation can immobilize you or make you deeply depressed or scared or sad. But you have two or three more decades when this energy will still be prevalent on the planet. However, when we tell you there is more light coming, we mean it. You will see the evidence of more light as you move through the coming years and decades.

Light will start to become more of a currency
on Earth than it has ever been able
or allowed to be.

Even though you find yourselves in unnerving times, you are in these unnerving times because what is heating up inside the Earth is burning through the Earth herself, and then will work its way through people, asking you to shed, shed, shed old energies. That is one way of giving you an overview of that which you are asking about.

DIANNA:

Where is the light coming from that's coming to the Earth more now than ever?

THE Z'S:

From two places: from inside the Earth herself — the energy that is being driven up to the surface and through the people — and also from the higher consciousness that the Earth is being forced into because of where energy is moving in a universal sense.

The Universe is going through its own
reshaping — or rebirth, if you like — and
Earth is a key planet in that rebirth
because Earth represents "heart."

This is why all manipulations of heart, all blocks to heart energy on Earth right now, are discordant to more of you than ever before, because those do not reflect the true energy signature of this planet.

Nonheart energy is part of the energy template or grid that was seeded on this planet that did not originate here and did not belong here before it was implanted. One positive side of how your grid was manipulated is that it got Earth beings (humans mostly) into a new place of awareness that perhaps they would not have reached so fast.

To understand where the light comes from, it can be helpful to think about gravity on Earth, which works in two ways: it roots you down into the planet from below, but it also keeps you contained in the sphere of the Earth, the Earth's energy field, as a force originating from above and around you. And light is coming onto the planet from above and around you as well — not necessarily light you can see, like sunlight or a ray of light, but instead a shift in the frequencies. Earth is no longer able to hold on to some of the density that it has been holding on to, for Earth is supposed to go through her transformation.

As key beings on this planet (humans), you are also going through a somewhat precarious transformation — the kind of transformation that for some of you feels like a death process at times. But that is appropriate, and that is how it is meant to be at this time on Earth as an experience.

DIANNA:

What made these crystals come online?

THE Z'S:

They have been online in many ways for thousands and thousands of years. But what started to happen in the twentieth century was this: Earth was able to start to move back to some of its "star origins." Meaning, the story of Earth had been, shall we say, dumbed down. The story of your origins as people, the story of Earth's history, was manipulated and modified and hidden from all of you. And your origins contain incredible power, more power than those who wanted to control humans (or again, "enslave" humans) were willing for you to see, know, or be. Because in the game of planetary warfare, it would not be convenient if Earth became too powerful.

DIANNA:

So, what are our origins that we need to remember?

THE Z'S:

That is not for this discussion. We must be a little mindful here of where the audience is willing and ready to go. If we started speaking to you about the entirety of your origins, we would need a full one to two hours, and it would take us in a completely different direction.

DIANNA:

Understood. I want to ask you about a mantra or a statement I read in a book. Please tell me if you think it is empowering. The book said it would be good for us to say, "I'm a human being becoming. Help me become. I'm a human being becoming. Help me become." It's reaching out to the greater Universe to support this journey to the new human soul. Is this correct?

THE Z'S:

"Correct" is an interesting word. We appreciate you bringing that up because there is a notion of "correct" or "incorrect" on Earth, as we have already discussed a few times. Things are very right/wrong, black/white in the thinking on Earth. The biggest problem is, none of that is true. There is no right/wrong, black/white. There is perspective. There is multidimensionality. Until you are all allowed to include that in your thinking again, you will always feel limited. You are all coming out of sleepwalking when it comes to your potential and reconnecting with the vastness of everything. And to your question, we will say: Was that sentence correct in that book for all the readers who read it, who found their way to it? And at the time it was put into that book, was it a good, high vibration for people? Yes. Will it still be so in decades to come? For the right reader, yes. How would our version of that mantra go? Our version would go something like this: "I am a human soul becoming. I am remembering. I am divine. I allow my soul energy back through me."

"Help" is a tricky word. Sometimes help is your savior. So, in those cases when you say, "Help me!" it can come from a very open-hearted place where you are reaching across to another person or place to receive something that will uplift you. But in other cases when you say, "Help me!" you are in what we would call the "victim state"; you are believing you are "less than." So, the statement that you just read to us would be very good for people who had come through a lot of religious programming. Because in religion, you are taught in subliminal and overt ways that you are separate from God, not connected to God. It is often coming from a very hierarchical standpoint. Now, God is what people make of it. There are some who believe God is a mystical force. There are some who believe God is a female form. Some believe it is a male form.

Notice how religion has conveniently been a wonderful mask for war on the planet. War is the great seduction on Earth, and it is the great destroyer of oneness. Religion and war, if you notice, have been long interlinked. What a number was done on humanity to entice them to feel a little of their soul by giving them highly organized and controlled religion, and then to allow war to also take place, and somehow link the two, so that people do not see the soul and war as separate. It is the ultimate "job" that was done on humans. Because if you link the soul and war, then the soul will never fully grow. Because the soul is trapped when it is under the influence of war. Equally, if you allow war to be associated with spirit and soul (such as in "holy wars"), you empower war. You give war an even more almighty power on the Earth.

Why is war convenient for those who wanted to keep humans in their place? Because war creates fear, destruction, devastation, and most importantly, separation. And separation is a war against oneness. With any of the separation you are seeing play out on your world stages right now (this is currently being done through politics or media, or how your news is reporting things), notice how you are all being asked to see certain groups or individuals as "less than."

Notice how hierarchical the whole story you are constantly told, over and over again, is. Again, we say this not to depress you. Some of you are already feeling a little alarmed or a little triggered as you're reading this, for you're starting to think the planet is a very dark place. We must tell you the planet is not a dark place. There are dark energies at work on this planet that have been here from way before you were born, so you were born into them. Now,

think of all the times that you have been in light or in love on this planet, and understand that those experiences are the truth of the soul energy and the spirit energy on Earth.

You are currently trying to excise some of these darker energies. So, what prompted us to speak to you about religion and war and how it has all been sewn together was the phrase "Help me!" because we want you to understand that as you go through your life, you are constantly going to change, evolve, and reconfigure those things that are useful to you. Children who are five play with each other in a certain way, but when they are thirty, and in the same group of people, they will not play with each other in the same way.

Now, don't get us wrong. The parents of that group will also then be older, and they will look at their thirty-year-old children all playing together, and they will be quite amazed by how they can still see the seeds of the energy of those little people that they knew when they were five. Now, they'll see them at thirty, and they'll still see evidence of who they were at five, but how those children are now exhibiting themselves and what they now want to "play" will be far more sophisticated, far more layered, and far more, shall we say, spread out.

Of course, you wouldn't call it "play," for most of you, as adults, think you're not playing. We would argue that you're always playing at life, even though it might not look or feel like a children's game. And let's not forget, children have quite peak-and-valley experiences. You humans often get this romantic idea about childhood. You look back on childhood, or you look at little children, and you think, "Oh, it's so innocent when you are a child." Actually, it's not! If you really are honest with yourself, go back to some of your earliest years on the planet, and think about the horror or the pain or the shock or the emotional reactions that were running through your body.

Very early on as a child, especially if you are open, you start to imbibe all of it. You start to feel the light. You start to feel the love. You start to feel the suffering. You start to feel the pain. You start to feel the abandonment. You don't like it when you feel the lower elements, and you start to react.

To circle all the way back to your first question on this, the reason we say that a phrase like "Help me!" can be wonderful for a certain person at a certain stage is because it can. We just want to remind you that words have power, and you all see words slightly differently. Even those of you reading this are having wildly different experiences in response to what we are saying. Some of you are hearing things that we haven't said. Some of you, if you report on this book to a friend, will say we said specific things that we did not say! If you go back and reread, you'll see that we didn't say them, but they're what you took away.

The reason we bring this up, Dianna, is part of your religious programming has made you all try to play spirit by the rules — rules that you've been given and handed by other people. It is very natural for all of you as you start to awaken to spirit again, awaken to your soul, to want to know, "Am I getting this right?" We hate to say this to you, but there is no "right"! There is what's right for you in the moment. And what's right for you in the moment will change and evolve and grow as you go. For some of those reading or listening, the mantra you first read out is highly appropriate today. For others, it would be wildly inappropriate at this stage of their journey. But that doesn't mean the mantra is "wrong."

That just means that you are very multidimensional people living at a time on Earth when you all need something slightly different at different times. The reason we have spent so much time trying to drive this home to you is,

words are power. And you need to constantly
refine your own words, and the words you
allow into your life, as your connection to

power changes. We do not mean power over
others. We mean the power of your heart,
the power of your soul, the power of
who you are here to be.

Words are a little like navigation. A map is not the destination you are going to, but without it, many of you would not find the destination you wanted to get to. Words are wonderful maps. And as your destination changes, as you progress further along your journey, you may need to update the map you are using. We hope that makes sense.

DIANNA:

It does. It goes back to our need to be responsible in making choices that serve us as individuals, and not just assume one thing fits everyone. I really appreciate you clarifying how important it is to know when words are being used to control us. We call those "directed" words. It could be as simple as, "It's going to be a horrible weekend. We might as well prepare. It's going to be a really bad weekend." Somebody programs us through the use of words.

I find when someone does that to me, I tend to go, "No, it's not. It's going to be a great weekend. Nope — it's going to be a great weekend!" I'll say it aloud and reverse it or make it exactly what I need it to be. I keep my focus on having a wonderful weekend — that's what I'm counting on. You brought up something important for us to consider with the use of words. I think we all need to be much more discerning and conscious of our choices of words and phrases, and who we use them with — children, adults. Children can get so confused based on the energy and the words that can be used around them. Do you have any thoughts on that?

THE Z'S:

A powerful and important example you just gave, Dianna. We will add this: The way that words can control you is by creating an emotion inside you. For example, if this person in your life says to you, "It's going to be a horrible weekend," you — in your reaction, in your mind, in your feelings — may suddenly feel sunk, suddenly feel scared, suddenly feel, "Oh no!" You are simply believing what you are being told. But you aren't believing the words; you are believing the reaction you're having. And the reaction you're having is what's going to create the future for you, not the words. But that is when certain words are designed to manipulate you or hold you down. And the key always is your reaction, your feeling. This is why we say to you, "Become aware of how you feel. Become aware of what you are experiencing." Because too many of you for so long have been asked to avoid how you feel and follow orders, follow instructions, follow the rules without thinking about whether it is jarring for your body.

When you start listening to your body, and discerning whether or not something feels true to you, you will begin to free yourself from the types of manipulation where someone else tells you what to think or how to feel.

What is very interesting to us is there are a growing number of people on your planet who are quite rightly seeing the manipulation in your media. They are beginning to notice how agendas are served. And people are not as stupid as the media would like you to believe they are. This is why you have had a bit more friction on Earth in response to some of the biggest news stories of the last few years. Division is being sewn; separation is being seeded.

And some people are buying it, hook, line, and sinker. They are completely believing what they are being told. But it is not the words they are believing. It is their emotional reaction. So, after reading a certain story, one person may be running around headlessly in fear because fear is what got activated in them. Meanwhile, someone else may feel completely differently about the story and be absolutely baffled as to why the other person is so hysterical. You see, this is where the power of your emotional energy fields comes into play. And because you are an emotionally immature planet, you are far easier to divide.

Now, the reason you are an emotionally immature planet is not because humans are inherently emotionally immature. You are emotionally immature as a people because your emotional maturity was restricted and taken away from you. Your growth was stunted. Wisdom, and spiritual wisdom in particular, helps create and enhance emotional maturity. People have been disconnected from their own spiritual wisdom, herded, and told what to think, what to believe, and what happened historically in order to shut down their potential. So they have become a people who are not as emotionally mature as they would be if they were allowed to come to their own relationship with wisdom — spiritual wisdom, human wisdom, whatever you want to call it.

So, Dianna, you pointing out what you just did in your response is *very* important because we cannot stress enough the importance of "word warfare" on Earth. The "word warfare" is not in the words themselves. It is in the reactions that you have to the words. The more aware you all become of your own inner reactivity to various things in your life, the more mature you can become, the less reactive you can become, the wider your energy field gets, and the more your soul becomes a part of the conversation on Earth.

We do understand that some of you wish it would hurry up. Some of you who are already less reactive in yourselves put a lot of focus on wishing that others on the planet were already that way too. Please stop wishing that! We only say that because we worry about you diminishing your own power and your own joy when you wish for that. That diminishment comes from wishing it away. If you are embodied in what we are describing, do you not understand that you are supposed to be an ambassador of that on the planet? We say that with love, not with judgment.

It will be very freeing for you to
believe us when we say this, and to finally
free yourself from this idea that something's
going wrong on the planet.

You knew exactly what you were incarnating into. Even those of you who spend too many hours a week telling all your spiritual friends, "Yes, I also wish I wasn't on this planet." That's actually a lie. If you were not supposed to be on this planet, you would be dead. We promise you that. It's very easy to die on this planet, very easy to exit. So, we ask you to stop sitting there quietly wishing everything else around you were different, because in doing that, you are dimming your power to change this planet into the kind of planet you want to see.

What is capable of making the vibrational difference? *You* are. So, if you are raising the vibration, how are you going to share that in the world, and be that in the world? By example, example, example. You all learn through energetic example. More people setting the example of vibrational difference is how the planet will change.

DIANNA:

I would call that "role-modeling," where people feel and see the other way to do something that maybe they hadn't thought of.

THE Z'S:

"Role-modeling" is a beautiful way of describing it because on a human level, that perfectly illustrates what we are driving at. And this leads to another aspect, Dianna, which is admiration. Admiration, when it is coming from a heartfelt place, is wonderful. It is you admiring a quality in another person or a way of being in them that you can separate from and attribute to them. For example, "Oh, my sister. She is so kind. She is always doing things for people. She is amazing." Is she? Or is she just being something you would like to be a bit more of yourself? Because you are amazing too, in a different way.

Be careful of separating yourself when it comes to admiring others that are role-modeling a way of being. You are only recognizing that way of being as good because you can feel the potential of it inside yourself. You might be amazed if you started acting a bit like your sister. The reason she's being kind is not to be some kind of saint or martyr or because she cares about other people admiring her. Other people admiring you is quite boring. It doesn't do a lot for you. It only feeds wounded egos. Unfortunately, anyone with a wounded ego who is constantly seeking admiration gets more and more lonely and compressed the more they don't heal the ego.

The more they get addicted to attention and admiration, the more painful it gets for them, and that is not a good place to be. You do not want to be an "admired" person, because that's none of your business. It does you no good. It doesn't feed you. You want to be a "connected" person. You want to be a person who is connected to others or who others feel connected to, and you will arrive at that by being yourself. This woman whose qualities you are admiring, maybe those are her gifts for the world, and you have different gifts.

That leads us to the other kind of admiration, the admiration that gets a little lower in vibration: jealousy, envy. *That* is when you are caught in a trap of admiring something you would like to be or like to have, and you immediately separate yourself from it. In separating yourself from it, you often decide to blame the person who has it or is it, as if it's their fault, whereas actually, it's completely your fault. We say that not to be horrible, but simply to be blunt. If you are caught in jealousy or envy, get out of it quickly! Because it's only going to bring you down, and it is simply a trap. In a way, though, jealousy and envy can be wonderful — wonderful signals to you that there is something you desire, something you admire and desire to be or have.

In an abundant, magnetic Universe, why don't you start directing some attention to allowing the qualities you admire to come to you? If you become jealous of another person, you hurt yourself more than you hurt them. We want you to understand that. We don't want you to be hard on yourself as you read this, horrified because you realize that jealousy or envy has been a big theme in your life. That's not your fault either. That's just inherited behavior. It's the "dis-ease" of being human that you have swallowed, the wound of jealousy that you have ingested that you are now replaying.

But here is the good news. If you are reading this with any awareness that this is true for you, this is a wonderful day! This is the day that you've figured it out! It might take you some months or years to really let jealousy or envy leave your system because it has become emotionally wired in you from many different incidents and people, and you might need a bit of time to fully let go of it. But as we said in one of the earlier conversations, awareness is your breakthrough. Awareness is to be celebrated. If you are aware of something of a lower vibration that you are doing in yourself or have done to others, and you are feeling remorse or shame about it, we ask you, please burn through those emotions as quickly as possible so that you can get back to realizing, "How wonderful that I have become consciously aware enough that I can now see something I did that was too small and perhaps hurt me or hurt someone else. How wonderful that my wisdom has grown to such an extent that I can see that now."

How's your self-love? Because that's the issue. If you aren't very loving toward yourself and you have not yet worked on loving, accepting, or forgiving yourself, you are going to struggle with judgment when you notice something you did or think you did that wasn't very good or was unkind. But if you have learned to work on loving yourself — being more compassionate with yourself, recognizing that being human is not easy and can be very problematic and very difficult, and sometimes very, very stressful on emotional and energetic levels — have compassion for yourself. All of you are doing the best you can, but sometimes you aren't doing as well as you could because you have been conditioned to be blind to some of your own distorted energetics. And no one has ever sat you down and spoken to you about the energetic knot that is jealousy or envy and unpacked that subject.

Of course, those who want you to live a lower-vibrational narrative will support that outcome. For instance, we'll again go back to your mainstream media. While there are some good news sources and some good journalists, if you look at the whole picture, you will see the low vibrational level and distortion that exist in the majority of stories. By all means, look at them, but look at them with awareness. Don't be blindly asleep when you read that stuff. That is how you ingest everything energetically in those stories that is designed to diminish you. Read it with a watchful eye. Observe how it makes you feel.

Look for the manipulative words in the articles that are telling you that you are supposed to be feeling a certain way. How dare they interfere with your sovereignty like that. Wake up and notice when you are being supported versus when you are being manipulated or diminished.

DIANNA:

Thank you. That's very empowering. It makes me think of a quote I took from "Soul Imprints," a recording you did recently on the art of transformation. In that recording, you give various soul-empowering phrases to say for just ten minutes, once a day, if that's all a person has time for. One self-empowering phrase that I think can speak to many of us is this one: "I allow myself to feel everything. I allow myself to release everything. I allow myself to become who I am here to be."

THE Z'S:

Yes, and we would like people to notice how they *felt* as they read those sentences or heard that recording. For some of you, you felt liberated and enhanced. But for some of you, the sentence "I allow myself to feel everything" put you straight into fear. You immediately panicked or worried that your feeling everything would mean you'd feel the worst. If that was your experience, it is good information. You can then ask yourself, "Are there things in my past or my present that I'm not willing to feel or that I haven't yet felt, and that is what I am avoiding? Or is that just my human conditioned mind trying to keep myself safe, not feel too much, telling me, *Don't do this, don't do that*?"

But what if you read that sentence, "I allow myself to feel everything," and you realized you were going to feel the highest levels of bliss, connection, and well-being that you ever have in your life? We will tell you this: those of you reading this, especially if you are still reading these conversations after experiencing many other transmissions from us, you are of a high-vibrational mind. The reason we have to tell you that is because (and this is important) only 10 percent of you had a positive and uplifting response to the words, "I allow myself to feel everything." Only 10 percent of you. And you are a high-vibrational group.

Now, that is not a reflection of you. That's a reflection of your planet. Very few people on the planet are free of the idea that their feeling everything could be not a bad thing, but a good thing. Most have been taught about the feelings they are supposed to fear. And very little teaching has been given on how to cultivate or open to good or high feelings. We don't mean hedonistic high feelings that don't last. We mean peace. We mean sustained well-being. We mean a sense of expansion.

Many of you now — more than ever before — are practicing that, which is wonderful. You're doing it through meditation. You're doing it through presence exercises. You're doing it through healing work. You're doing it through music. You're doing it through so many ways. But notice that you all have to give yourselves concentrated time each day when you cultivate that. And even those of you who are doing a lot of work in this area might spend only two or three hours of your sixteen to eighteen wakeful hours doing it.

The percentage of time that humans are currently allowed to feel expanded and in well-being is very low. Now, rather than let anything we have just said depress you, watch the way you react, and understand that any emotional reaction you have to anything can feed your beliefs, and your beliefs either impede or amplify your ability to manifest. Notice the reaction you've had.

Now, we want to take you back to something we referred to several minutes ago: the importance of your role on this planet. Not your role in the sense of how others perceive you or things they might compliment you on. No. If you are one of the high-vibrational people on this planet (and we have just laid out to you that even you have a certain limit on how much time you believe you can spend in well-being or peace or expansion — even you!), do you understand why you are needed? Do you understand how you cultivating that in and for yourself then emanates it into the world? That's very important for you to "get." Especially those of you who feel despair about what you see the planet going through right now, do not just sit and watch and react. Become the antidote.

*That is what you are all here to play out
in this transitionary time on Earth.
You are here to become the antidote
you think the Earth and people need.*

DIANNA:

So, if humanity is the collection of humans on the Earth, could you end our conversation today by explaining what a human is exactly? And are there different types of humans on this Earth?

THE Z'S:

Well, the humans that you are today are different from the humans that you were several thousand years ago, partly because of the influence of energetics and time and cultural factors. But also because (as we said) the Earth is currently in its most expanded state of the last three thousand years. The vibration of humanity has reached a height that was last present on this planet three thousand years ago. But even then, even when those high vibrations were present, the lower levels of the Earth were, in fact, far lower than the low now.

This is why we also hear many of you bemoaning what you see going on on Earth. We like to remind you that, in fact, many of you are having a far more comfortable experience on Earth than you have had in any of your previous incarnations. We understand that might seem odd to you, for you are so focused on what you are bothered by. But in truth,

you are having one of the highest experiences
on Earth that has ever, in fact,
been possible for human life.

We say that so that you will really sit with it and allow it in.

As for who humans are now, they are now a little more of a "hybrid" than they used to be. Meaning, there was a time when human density was a lot more fixed and the human mind and emotions were not as open — certainly not multi-dimensionally open — as they are now. Humans have come a very long way, and you all have different roles. Some of you have studied the archetypes that you have learned through-out ancient history, and you can see archetypes inside your-self and those around you. You can see that you might be a little bit more the archetype of the leader, or you might be a little bit more the archetype of the supporter.

But what we want all of you to understand is, the time when archetypes were a good guide for humanity has passed. They're still important and they can still be included, but what all of you are able to do and become now is more than you ever were before. Perhaps in the sixteenth century, un-derstanding your archetype was useful. But at this point, those of you who are having an expanded experience as a soul, you are going to go through at least eight archetypes in your life, though maybe not all at once. Some of you will do them one at a time, and you will embody a new archetype as you go through each new transformation cycle.

There are many different types of humans, but there are more different types of souls. Again, as we have said, the soul animates the human, and there are those souls who are here on Earth as "transmitters." They might be a little more ele-mental, or you might experience them as a little more airy, a little less fixed in their thoughts or their ways or their being, but they transmit energy. These are people who, when you are in their presence, you feel a strong current of air moving through them.

Then there are those who are here to forge. They are very earthbound. They are almost rocklike. They are the kind of beings who you might say "get things done," but often, they are not people who are going out there and getting things done themselves. They are just bringing out the element of rock and strength that is in their energy field. So, they often pair up with people who are good at going out there and structuring things, and their rocklike energy and presence affect those who are trying to create something and help ground and stabilize it.

Then there are those humans who are here for the mystical. These might be people who you know privately or publicly as healers, as sages, as those who bridge the spirit world to humanity.

Then there are those souls and humans who are here to help the *bodies* of humans. You often see these people go into healthcare. You often see them become naturopathic healers. They are here to work on and with the body of other humans. Then there are those human guardians whose job it is to tend to nature. They're here to either repair nature, be a voice for nature, or be in union with nature. Then there are those humans who are here to work with the animal kingdom.

And so on, and so on. We could keep going. We could give you over thirty examples of this, but here is the point: all of you have at least four to eight of these leanings. You may not be a health worker or healer, but your fourth or fifth leaning might be in that arena. You are perhaps fascinated by health. You, maybe, see this as your hobby. It's not your job. It's not one of the first two or three things that you are in the world.

Perhaps first you are a parent. Then you are a lawyer, and you are helping work on justice because those who go into law are always interested in the energetics around justice, some more evolved than others. Some like the fight around justice. Some like the truth around justice. And some like to play with justice. You see, in every single individual area that humans are archetypally lined up with, there are many different ways that they could be playing with that archetype.

So, when we say to you that you may first be a parent, second a lawyer, and third a lover or a partner, we don't just mean a partner to your beloved; we mean you are the kind of person who can emanate warmth and intimacy to anyone in ways that surprise some people, for they don't even experience that kind of intimacy with their spouse. So, when they meet you, perhaps they're taken aback, or they reject you or push against you.

But your fourth leaning may be health. In this life, you decided not to come in as a healer or a health worker, but you are fascinated by health. It is your hobby. It is your passion, and it's what you tell other people about. You see, all of you have many different archetypes within you. And this is a time in history when most of you will master and embody at least eight.

We have often said that each enlightened human being exhibits eight areas of mastery. One area of mastery might be a mastery of peace and diplomacy. One area of mastery might be a mastery of music. One area of mastery might be a mastery of love. And once you have mastered eight areas, you step into what you would call "enlightenment."

It is a little like unlocking levels of a game. Once you have that harmonic circle of eight areas operational in your energy field, you start to live from a more enlightened space because you have reclaimed and reenergized more parts of your soul than the human training ever encouraged or allowed you to. You have risen above, and you have become enlightened. You have entered light. You are living more in the light of yourself and the light of existence than you were before.

When we tell you that mastering eight areas is going to put you into a state of enlightenment, remember, many of you have a very fixed idea about what you think enlightenment is. We ask you to reserve that judgment until you *are* in that state. For you start telling yourself it should look like this person or that person — but it will look different in every person who embodies it. But it is a sense of flow, peace, well-being, and an ability to very quickly return to a state of presence, even if you are taken out of that for a period of time.

Enlightenment is when you don't lose the light
of life for very long. You are able to cultivate
light, maintain it, and emit it into the world.

So, when we tell you that you have the opportunity to master eight aspects of your humanity in this lifetime, understand that we are saying you are here to have a spiritually enlightened life and seed that energy on the planet.

DIANNA:

That's a beautiful reminder, and I think we'll end our conversation here today. Thank you, Z's.

THE Z'S:

Good. Thank you. Thank you to all in this conversation, for you who are reading are part of it. Ha! "How does that work?" you say. "We weren't in the room!" Well actually, you were! Because we have been tapping into the coming fifty years for this conversation and sensing those of you who might be wanting to hear certain things. And because Dianna has been doing the same, energetically, psychically. And because of the connection that we are in with her and with all of you.

We will say again something we have said before: If you read this conversation more than once, you will realize you are reading a different conversation each time. And if you don't quite get that, or are a little mystified by that, we will tell you the secret to it: You are listening multidimensionally. Which means you are a multidimensional being, remembering that you are. And conversations like this are designed to reactivate that memory inside you.

In peace and in love to all.

Chapter Two

CONVERSATION FIVE

Topics

- The journey of the brain, mind, and heart
- The spiral nature of universal information
- The nature of the lower, middle, and higher mind
- The imprint of self-judgment
- The soul's connection to the body
- New technologies and the brain-mind-heart connection
- The heart is in charge — it is the leader, the sun, the power source
- Heart energy is the most important resource on Earth at this time
- The nature of oneness in a multidimensional Universe

CONVERSATION FIVE

DIANNA:

Welcome back to *Conversations with the Z's*. This is conversation five. Welcome, Z's.

THE Z'S:

Good. Welcome. A pleasure to be back in the relay of this conversation.

DIANNA:

Today, I want to address a question that I know the answer to because you've spoken about it before. I want to take us on a journey — the journey of brain, mind, heart. Who's in charge? I'd like to take some time to move on to understanding how our greater communication skills work. Could we start with our brains? I feel that we have little understanding of how our brains really work. As a kid, I thought it was a giant file cabinet where I stored everything I learned. But I realized later in life that our brains aren't this finite space. I feel that the brain is more of a receiver and transmitter of information and that the brain communicates with every cell in the body, and every cell in the body also transmits and receives messages. So, could we get into a conversation about what the brain is?

THE Z'S:

Well, a couple of different aspects need to be addressed here. Firstly, the brain is (as you have said) far more than it has previously been understood to be. The concept of the brain as a transmitter is very much a fact when it comes to psychic information and your ability to connect with the realms around you. Your brain is capable of taking in information that comes from outside you and helping you to process it. That is one part. But the bigger part about the brain is, it is the key to the existence of the human body.

Think of the heart. We are specifically speaking here about the heart chakra, not the organ — the heart chakra, which sits in the center of your chest. In many ways, this is your soul. So,

if you wanted to find a part of your body
that most represented your soul essence,
it would be the heart, the heart chakra.

This is where the oneness inside you resides. This is why many of you speak about your heart when you are speaking about love, caring, feeling connected. It is your connection center. Yet, we will tell you that the brain is crucial. For the brain is running the show in the body far more than people realize or give credence to.

If your brain is out of balance, it will put everything out of balance. You could say the brain is the body's "third eye," and of course, it is more than that. It is running and maintaining all kinds of vital processes in the body. The brain and heart are, in fact, the most important aspects for a human being when it comes to being in contact with their soul energy and with what we would call "spirit" or "spiritual energy."

Again, this brings us back to what we have said all along: you are connected to all that is, and your human training has been to disconnect you from that truth. The awakening of your soul is to reconnect you to that truth. And so, the brain has the potential to become even more elevated in the decades to come. The brain has the potential to become even more in touch with what you might refer to as the "psychic realms" and to become even more of a transmitter. Think of your brain as your internet system. Inside yourself, it is the place where you have the ability to access so much. It is also the architect for you. For you put the architecture for your life into motion, forward movement, and structure by using the power of your brain. That is just a brief overview.

DIANNA:

Thank you. So, if brains are transmitters and receivers, where is all this information going and coming from? I believe exactly what you said — that the technology we see today is a representation of how our brains work, the system works, our humanness works. And from a computer standpoint, I jokingly call it "the web of consciousness." Some people call it "the field," "universal source energy," "oneness," "one mind." Where is all this information going and coming from?

THE Z'S:

The question is not, "Where is it going and coming from?" It is more, "How are you able to stand in the middle of it and let it pass through you?" We understand that from a linear perspective and a human perspective, you are always trying to understand the beginning and the end of something, but from the perspective of spirit, there is no beginning and end. We understand that sounds obtuse. We do not mean to be obstructive to your question or your understanding, but that is simply the best way we can describe it to you. We have said before that energy moves in spirals and that time is a continuum, to the point where we cannot tell you the end of time. For we are here experiencing a version of time, just as you are. It is very different from the time that you experience as a human, but we cannot tell you where the ending is.

What we can tell you is that everything is passing through, moving through, and you also are passing through. So, instead of seeing it as quite so linear, we would ask you to see it as a little more spiral-like. You are a spiral, spiraling through countless spirals of universal information, energy, and understanding.

You spoke about the web of consciousness, and we would like to draw your attention to something here. Yes, the internet is a very powerful force on Earth. In fact, we will tell you that had the internet not come along at the time that it did, things could have been a lot darker on Earth at this time. For the internet helped to open the minds and also in many cases the hearts of people around the world. Before, you somewhat had blinders on as to what was going on in other places.

However (and this is important to understand), right now with your internet, you can see the exact same attempts to control, manipulate, and modify your ability to interact with the web of consciousness. It is a mirror of the web of consciousness. But just as the web of consciousness on Earth has been interfered with by human agendas and those who wish to be in power, so the internet has become its own new battleground when it comes to people trying to control it. You are seeing that right now. We are speaking in part about censorship, which is an important issue to consider and to notice. It is important that humans notice what is being censored and why, and ask those questions, rather than just simply complying or feeling sad about things going missing. You have to ask yourself, "Why, and by whom, and for how long has this been playing out?"

We have spoken to you before of the rise in consciousness on Earth, and we will tell you two things about your internet: it will have an updated system; and we see a high probability that it will be known by a different name in the coming decades. "The internet" will no longer be referred to. It will be important to adjust the name. Even though there are agendas to try and use your internet against you as a people — like many of the web of consciousness manipulations that are in attempt right now on Earth and have been for centuries — much of it is backfiring because the rise in power and heart and mind of people (because of their interaction with this technology) is strong and is happening rapidly. We don't mean people becoming mentally educated about what is going on in other places. What we mean, which is often not noticed by you as a people, is how it is altering the way that you all perceive, sense, and take in information. And when we say "information," we include emotion and sensory experiences. We don't just mean facts and words.

The reason that we address this is, the internet is one of the most powerful forces for change that you have right now, and it is not going anywhere in a hurry, but it will (in time) go through an overhaul, as will many of the world systems. And when you all decide it is time to update some of what you were given, as you go through these major transitions on Earth in the next decade or two, you are going to want to update, modify, and rebirth several of the names too (for names have a power and a vibrational energy) so that they can move forward into the higher consciousness that will exist in the future, and not stay in the lower-consciousness implants that you are currently dealing with.

In the previous conversation, when we spoke to you about the manipulation of media, we asked you to pay attention to when an article that you were reading was asking you to feel a certain way or telling you how you should feel about something. That is interfering with universal law. Universal law allows you as a sovereign being to be free, to have your own experience, to have your own perspective. Manipulative words are used to direct the attention and vibration of the uninitiated into a downward spiral of energy. And by "the uninitiated," we simply mean those of you on Earth who have never considered what we are saying or been taught to consider it.

This is why we say that certain things will be renamed. There are names for certain parts or aspects of your society right now that are very low vibrational (and deliberately so), in order to keep people thinking that's all that is possible for them. One of the greatest dis-eases or impediments hampering human empowerment right now is, you as a people do not realize how much possibility there is inside you individually or collectively. And that is not your fault. That is by design. That has been encoded.

You have been taught to consider "crazy" or "conspiratorial" anything outside the mainstream narrative that has been wired into your system. The battle against witches, for example, had very little to do with witchcraft and very much to do with control of powerful women — women who were about to influence the masculine to become more divine because those women were coming into their power. Not only were a group of those women castigated, and many of them murdered (as well as some men who were considered to be involved in what was branded "witchcraft"), but a very dark story was also created around witchcraft, making people afraid of witches and what they can do. And then (and this is the hidden power in what happened there) other women were made afraid of being a witch because of murder.

This manipulation was very subtle. Not many stand back and look at that story and realize that it, and events like it, caused part of their fear of spirit or fear of any kind of magic or power that they might be connected to. As a result, because they have an ancestral and an informational memory that many beings who were apparently practicing "dark art" were murdered, that magic or power in them is subconsciously blocked from happening. And remember, the human animal is designed to respond to fear or threat. If the fear energy gets going in a human, they lose touch with their rational mind. They hook out of their own brain, their own mind, their own ability to process (this goes back to your original question, Dianna), and they lose contact with spiritual truth. They start to only listen to their lowest emotions and be guided by their lowest emotions.

This is why vibration is so vital. We know that many of you who have been spiritual students for a long time — activated, awake seekers — get a little bit bored of hearing us or other people telling you to raise your vibration; it feels like a job, it feels like homework. It's a bit like being told to wash your face six times a day! But the reason we tell you this is,

vibration is everything. And the level
of vibration that you achieve, maintain,
and cultivate inside yourself dictates the world
you create for yourself and others.

The world is not held in lower-vibrational thinking or feeling. Imagine the potential when all these highly intuitive brains and hearts come online and reconnect to their spirit. The power of humanity to awaken and arise is profound. And that power is slowly but surely manifesting itself. We know these times are a little, we will say, "edgy" and difficult for you to navigate as you watch some of these lower-vibration inflictions happening to certain people (and often to people who are blissfully unaware they are happening). That is challenging for you, yes. But understand, humanity is more powerful than those lower agendas at this time. And humanity is not doing it all by itself. The rise in consciousness is real, and the rise in consciousness will raise each human being.

DIANNA:

Thank you for that explanation. While we're still on this topic of brain/mind, could you move to explaining what the mind is? Because you mentioned what happens if we lose our rational mind. So, what is the mind?

THE Z'S:

Well, we will put it this way to you: You have a lower mind and a higher mind. And of course, you have everything in between, but we will put it in those terms because it will be easiest to understand. Think of your mind as a cinema or movie theater screen and the brain as the projector. The mind is where you receive the projected thoughts, emotions, memories, images. It is a little bit like playing the movie of your life every single day. And sometimes the movie and the soundtrack of the movie recall past moments that were difficult or joyous and bring them in. And other times the mind is a little more open to the new. When you are in the lower mind, you tend to be mostly tracking past negative thoughts or emotions. When you are in the higher mind, you are open and able to transmute many of these lower or past or heavier thoughts or feelings, and you are willing to be touched by the now, willing to connect to the now.

The mind, in many ways, can be seen as an auric field. Imagine you were looking at a human being and you could see the brain inside their head. (We know that's a little unusual, but remember we are doing a visual exercise here.) Now imagine the mind as an auric field around the top half of the head. This is the place where dreams, desires, fears, and hopes all play out. They are, in a way, interpreting for you what is happening in your life and where you want to go; the mind is a very important guide for you.

We will give you an example of the "higher mind" here: Lee, like many on Earth who are intuitive or open to their channeled beings and guides, is able to access his higher mind very quickly. It doesn't mean he is always living in it. He also has his lower mind and his medium mind, just like all of you, because he has to work through all the levels in himself. But the higher mind is where you are able to open to higher information, higher intuition. And remember, when we refer to "higher," all we mean is, "connected." You often think of higher mind as this unique spot above your own mind that has nothing to do with anyone else.

We have explained to you that we are eighty-eight beings that then also connect into the wider Universe, and Lee is connecting with us. Some of you might imagine this channeling experience he is having as quite linear; you are hearing a group of guides coming through Lee's body. Sure, you can look at it that way, and that way works, but actually, what you are witnessing is someone expanding their consciousness into greater consciousness itself.

It would be a little strange for Lee, or for any of you at this time in history, if there weren't a group of guides that were filtering higher consciousness through to you. For remember, you still identify with the body, individuality, and connection. But there can come a time in human history when you are no longer accessing higher consciousness through the filter of guides, and you are simply connected to all that is, without any bridge. We aren't saying one way is better than the other, please understand; we are just giving you a bigger picture around the whole thing.

Are the mind and the brain deeply connected, working in harmony? Yes. But think of the mind as the projection screen that does not exist in the brain; the brain does not have that level of auric field awareness. The brain instead projects and transmits these pictures and these thoughts into an auric field above and around your head, which, again, is the mind. But your mind can also connect up and above, and beyond, and around. So, when you are in the higher mind, you are able to connect far beyond your programming.

When you are in the lower mind, you tend to be working through who you have been programmed to be and what your programming has been. There is no need to go to the lower mind if you are not in the past. And we know that can confuse some of you, for you think, "Can I not just be a little sad in the present and have feelings that exist in the present?" Well, not really, because those feelings come from human ancestry. So, even if you are having a true present-moment experience of sadness that you can't place in your own personal history in this lifetime — for example, you can't remember the time that you felt this sad before or what the trigger was — understand you are playing out and trying to clear ancestral, emotional human programming that you were born into, rather than something you experienced in this lifetime through your body.

Many of you like to think of your bodies as the carriers of this information. We would say, normally the body accounts for 20 to 25 percent of the ancestral memories you carry. The rest is learned energy once you incarnate. Even if you don't know your birth parents, you will still be carrying some imprint, and as we said, it's usually no more than 20 or 25 percent of their ancestral and your genetic line. But the biggest influence for you once you incarnate will be all the people around you in the early years, and more specifically, not just them as people but what they themselves have imbibed and been working with. Because no individual human is, in fact, an individual. That is one of the hardest things for some people to get their heads around.

DIANNA:

Thank you. Given the limitations of our language, I thought that was an excellent explanation for our future conversations around mind, body, and heart, so I appreciate that.

You talk about this lower mind, and the higher mind, and the middle mind, and I know it's just a paradigm we're trying to create here, an image. When Lee and I work with people, we're both very focused on getting them to understand the things that drive them (much of what you just explained — some inherited, some learned): their thoughts, their beliefs, their perceptions. You said the lower mind might be where people are holding on to these items that are holding them back. If we were to work with someone, would it help (do you think) if we said, "Let's separate the lower mind from the higher mind," just to give them a sense of freedom, in a way? Then they could look at their beliefs and perceptions that their lower mind is holding on to from a more objective and possibly safer-feeling place. How could we work with this image you just gave us?

THE Z'S:

Giving them that kind of scale and that kind of understanding to be able to notice the variance in themselves would be an excellent guide for most people, because people enjoy scales on Earth, and it is how many of you have been allowed to understand progress, which is good. But you have to be careful when you first present this to people. When you do it, watch how upset people get when they start to understand the principle of "OK, I have a lower mind, I have a higher mind." Watch how upset they get at themselves when they're telling you about the lower mind and realizing that it even exists. Remember, self-judgment runs strong on Earth. It shouldn't. Meaning, self-judgment is something that was implanted to keep you small, but unfortunately, not enough people on the planet are yet aware of it as a force that can cloud judgment, cloud possibility, cloud potential.

Pay attention to their reaction to the idea they have a lower mind, and try to encourage them out of the negative thinking around it. For example, your feet are the lowest part of your human body, but without your feet, how would you move around the world? And if you are someone who does not have feet, or legs, or part of your legs, then choose the lowest point on your body to understand that lower is not necessarily bad, but lower is where you get trapped. It is very hard to trap someone when the higher mind is active, but it is easy for the individual to get trapped in the lower realms because they have such a density of gravity and pull people down. But — and this is very important for everyone listening, reading, absorbing what we are saying, to understand — the lower is important to the clearing of Earth.

Many of you think you are coming here to create a higher plane. And yes, that is true, but part of the way that you are doing that is to actively engage with and clear the lower.

We understand the higher might feel nicer or feel better, particularly for those of you who are (what we would call) half in and half out of the human body. Meaning, there's half of you in the human body because you have to be, but the other half of you is mightily pissed that you even incarnated in the first place. Many of you are running that story. Again, we'll tell you to be careful of that judgment because you are again labeling something as "wrong" and something else as "right." And those are difficult paradigms for you to get free from as human beings. But they're important paradigms.

Where many of your minds will go now is, "Hang on a second. It's not nice to murder somebody. Surely, that's wrong." We would say to you that murder is a very low-vibrational act; it is an act of violence, war, and aggression. Sometimes that is something people play out. And if we were to put all of you through your paces when it comes to your incarnated lives, some of you would be horrified at the things that you did in other lifetimes because you're judging them from the now. But understand you have all been moving through an energy cycle. Again, it is very hard for us to address this without starting to get caught up in your human web of judgment about all of this.

So, Dianna, back to your question. Would that be a good way of framing it to somebody? Absolutely. And what you are encouraging them to do is to notice the energy ocean that moves through them every day, and

> *that is the most powerful thing anybody can*
> *do — become aware of their ups and downs.*
> *Not judge the fact they have downs — that's*
> *a trap — but just to become aware of their*
> *ups and downs and to know when it's*
> *a good time to make a decision.*

If you make many decisions when you are in a "down phase" and you start to notice they are catastrophic, then you start to learn, "Ah, I shouldn't make decisions when I'm in that state. In that state, I need to help myself heal, be soothed, rest," whatever it is. You're all learning your way as you go. We do enjoy that you bring this forward, Dianna, for what is important is trying to give people ways to become more aware of the wave of energy moving through them, and how to better work with it through becoming conscious of it.

DIANNA:

I appreciate that, because for the past thirty years, I've been very focused in my work around helping people look at the story they're telling themselves and the story they're manifesting. Doing that requires people to get real about just what we said — their beliefs, their perceptions, and so forth — and really get aware of the story and realize they have the power to change their story.

I hit a lot of blocks and hurdles as there is often a lot of resistance about letting go of your story, because it feels safe. It
may be a harmful story, from my perspective as I watch them,
but to them, sometimes it's more frightening to give up the
story and take responsibility for a new one. So, I appreciate
you giving me a new model to work with. Models are never
perfect. But sometimes one model will speak to someone in
a way another model did not. And for any therapist, or for
someone working just for their own self, it might be fun for
them to play with this very notion. So, I really appreciate that.

THE Z'S:

We appreciate you bringing up the idea that people are
afraid of their higher mind and their higher vibrations.
That goes back to what we have said about the training on
Earth, and the comfort and, we will say, "patterning" that you
have been given as a people around staying in low vibrations. But equally, the fear that has been sewn into you about
your own connection to spirit, the possibility of you connecting to magic, the possibility of other realms existing and
you being part of them — none of you have been given good
parenting around any of that. And if you aren't given
good parenting around any of that, where are (to use your
words, Dianna) your role models, or your guides, or those
that help you more easily become the thing that you aspire
to be when you first see and recognize it? So, if you scrub
out people's stories of their higher experiences, higher mind,
then people stick to what they feel safe in, but more than
that, what they feel traumatized by.

Trauma energy is a very magnetic energy, and it is an energy field that holds people in place. Although awareness of it has been growing on the planet considerably in the past few decades, there is still a lack of awareness of how trauma can limit and hold the body in place so that the body can no longer progress as it is designed to. And when we say, "the body," we of course also mean the soul. Now that there is more understanding of trauma, the trauma is beginning to become a little less comfortable. But when you weave in aspects like shame, self-judgment, self-hatred, and secrecy, then trauma becomes a recipe for destruction. Because if the humans are taught to feel those things around anything they feel traumatized by, if they are taught to be ashamed about their lower vibrations and aren't allowed to talk to others about them, the humans remain trapped.

It is why so much of the work in what you would call "healing work" or "healing workshops" or "healing activities" involves letting go of the lower dimensions. And there is nothing wrong with that. Sometimes there is a judgment on Earth that you're going to a healing workshop to get rid of that nasty piece of you that's in the way, and even seeing it that way is damaging to your progress. We are not judging anyone who is doing that right now or has done that, for that's normal; it's part of the culture. In fact,

when you are shedding those lower vibrations,
all you are doing is making space for the
higher to come in.

So actually, at this time in human history, working on clearing out lower aspects of yourself is one of the smartest things you can do. It is a little more "fashionable" or, we would say, "enjoyable" to work on developing your higher aspect, for when you connect there, you get in touch with a much higher and more spacious sense of yourself, and that is wonderful. That is the signature of home. You get to go back toward oneness in a more powerful way than ever before. But the more you excavate from the body the training and energy that have been, we will say, implanted there that keep you small, or low, or tightly held, the more you allow the higher in. So, doing that work of clearing out the lower is what some of you would call "God's work."

DIANNA:

If the soul never judges, and the self-judgment imprint that we carry keeps us away from our soul, where did this imprint of self-judgment come from, and is there anything else you want to say today about how we overcome it?

THE Z'S:

Self-judgment always takes you back to separation. You are either separating from yourself or from another.

If you are judging another person, you are separating from them; you are pointing the finger or judging their behavior and disconnecting from them because you don't like what you are actually in resonance with, in their lower vibration. What we mean by this is, often people will judge an aspect of another person that they have not yet become conscious of in themselves. For example, "Oh, I can't stand my friend Jennifer. She is so harsh on people." And in that moment, of course, what are you doing when you are saying, "I can't stand my friend Jennifer. She is so harsh on people"? That is a very asleep-at-the-wheel version of judgment, where you are completely unconscious of the obvious parallel you are manifesting by judging the person you think you are superior to, when in fact what you are trying to do is separate from that lower vibration in yourself.

Sometimes the judgment comes from the heart. You don't like suffering or pain, and you certainly don't want to see suffering or pain inflicted upon someone you love. You see this with parents a lot. It can be very hard for parents to forgive anyone who hurts or wounds their child because the parents have taken it upon themselves to try and protect the child from the world. The parental responsibility line is tricky, because once a child arrives — especially when the child reaches the age of twelve to fourteen and onward — the parent can no longer protect the child in such an effective way because the child is beginning to walk out into the world energetically and have their own experiences in a bigger way. They are drawn to learn the lessons they're drawn to learn, not just because of their parenting and their family lessons that they are trying to heal or grow beyond, but also because they have come here with their own mission, their own soul imprint, their own things to learn.

A parent who can truly forgive another being who hurts or wounds their child is in the higher mind. To any of you parents who are reading or listening and feeling torn because you yourself are dealing with this right now and you cannot or will not forgive, we are not saying you have to be happy that somebody hurt or wounded your child — not at all. That's completely different. But when you want to judge, attack, or take revenge upon someone who has hurt or wounded your child, you are caught in the early-parental responsibility. But your responsibility is supposed to evolve in you as the child grows, and particularly as they go through the teenage years and beyond.

In order for you to truly be their ally, their friend, and their new level of guardian in their adult life, it is going to be very important for you to understand that you no longer own them. They are not yours anymore. They are not yours to protect. It is not that you will not do your best to lovingly protect them — we are not saying you should not offer that. But the reason we are bringing this up is, so many of you get caught into judgment traps where you are separating from others.

And where did you learn separation from spirit and from others? We spoke about this in a prior conversation. It has been sewn into your collective. You were given a story of your history. You were indoctrinated with myths and stories from childhood, and all the way through the generations, you have heard the same stories over and over again. And much like we said about the media, if you look for the manipulation in those stories, you'll find it.

And your government is going through a huge revolution in this coming century. Are your governments overprotective parents whose role it is to shepherd and shield you? Or are your governments part of you, the people, and you are the electors of these people to help guide your systems? There has arisen an almighty imbalance and gap in that relationship.

If you want to look at an unhealthy relationship on Earth, consider the low level of evolution between leaders and those being led. Why is there such a gap in that grouping? You have to ask yourself that question. And again, we would like to say this: there are some very good people who are trying to lead their countries. There are some very good-natured, good-hearted politicians. We are not in any way pointing at individuals here. We don't want you to get into singling out this president or that prime minister, for that is its own kind of trap, and that's an illusionary way of looking at it that you've also been fed: "Let's find the one person who is to blame." Well, that is far less effective than looking at the system as a whole and understanding why the system itself is somewhat poisoned.

To go back to your original question, this was all sewn into the Earth template a long time ago — we spoke about this in the last conversation — and you are now getting to the point where you are beginning to question why this was sewn in. We could (of course) — and we are willing to — do a whole section on galactic history with you at some point, but the problem is, that information will not help you rise above or overcome self-judgment.

Understanding what it is, understanding how it infects and destabilizes you, and understanding how to rise above it is how you change it. People do not know how to build something because they are given a manual. People know how to build something because they start using a manual to try and put this thing together. Putting together a new way is actually far more important than understanding how you got into these problems in the first place.

DIANNA:

Thank you. I agree. I see that in my client sessions when they get trapped in the old story and don't want to focus their energies, talents, and gifts on creating a new story. We're going to go into that in other conversations, and also as we talk about death and dying. There are many "old stories" around the subjects of death and dying that limit people. I'm a huge believer in the need to normalize the conversation around death and dying. And talking about that subject will probably be a couple of conversations not too far from now.

THE Z'S:

We will do a whole body of work with you on the spiritual power of death, dying, and reincarnation.

DIANNA:

I'm really looking forward to that. And in the meantime, I want to go back to the brain/mind, and I want to tie it into some things that we see today in technology. I want to ask: If the brain and mind are overcome — you mentioned ways that they can be overcome — can the heart chakra still function and stay connected to the soul?

THE Z'S:

Yes and no. It becomes very difficult. We will put it this way: In a prior conversation, we said to you that once the soul connection to the body is so dimmed, so small that it is almost about to disappear (we will not say "snubbed out," for that implies that someone else did it to you), *that* is the point when you start to negotiate about leaving the planet. For if your soul cannot animate your human body, you are no longer here on a soul level.

There are some groups wherein people believe that the soul of a human can be removed, and a human can carry on as somewhat of a "robot." There aren't many of those, but there are a few groups who are trying those agendas right now; they will not succeed, but they will try. You can completely destabilize somebody's connection to their heart or, as we have said, their soul by overwhelming, overloading, or over-stimulating their mind. This is why some of the weapons that are used on Earth are not weapons that any of you would understand as weapons historically — meaning, unlike a gun, which everybody knows is a weapon. But there are so many other weapons that people who have these agendas can use.

Again, we have to be careful how far we go here because what tends to rise in you is fear. You hear this kind of thing, and your bodies start to go into fear, and *that* is where you get disabled. But the reason to bring this up with you is, there are many agendas on Earth where there is a lack of consideration of the soul or heart.

We will tell you that a good way to assess a leader on your planet is to see if they speak from or with their heart or not.

And by the way, there are some who are very good at giving you a little bit of heart and feeling somewhat convincing that they care, and then all of a sudden, dropping in a new piece of information that is clearly not so caring.

This is a little bit of a game of tic-tac-toe. If you praise someone twice, they might not notice that you are undermining them in the third sentence or action because they are seduced by the praise. So, the reason we ask you to look for heart connection, heart vibration in any leader that you are choosing to elect or bring into power is, *that* is the leadership of the future. You are not there yet. You are, right now, in the battle between the old and the new, and that is going to take a good few decades to fully play out. We are not saying that it's a few more decades that will look exactly like it does now; we are just saying it will take time for the energy signature on the planet to fully shift that way.

But you are, right now, at a point in history when there are certain ideas about how advanced you can become as human beings. But pay attention! It's not very advanced if somebody else is in charge of the advancement.

Advancing human beings is actually allowing them to come online in their consciousness.

If you are being given something that is human-created that is supposedly going to advance you, be very afraid. Be very wary and ask lots of questions as to what its creator wants to do with this piece of equipment that they are promising you advancement with. Pay close attention to the signature of their energy. Do you see heart, do you see compassion, do you see greater understanding? We're not talking about charm or charisma here, for those are quite surface energies; they do not run deep. And you know the difference between a certain level of charm or charisma and a true, heartfelt integrity.

That is going to be one of the chapters that you are facing in this next decade. You are facing a chapter of certain human beings telling you how you will be advanced by their technology, their agenda; and you should be very circumspect about any of those. It is very important to walk in with many questions.

DIANNA:

Well, thank you, because that's a perfect segue into what I wanted to ask you about next. I would encourage people to see any of the recent work of Gregg Braden. The one I got to see was from June 2019, from a GaiaSphere event — that's through Gaia TV. He is extremely well spoken on this very subject and offers a lot of examples and a lot of science. Anybody interested in this, I would encourage them to get more data for themselves.

THE Z'S:

Gregg is an excellent example of unified heart and scientific mind.

DIANNA:

He really is — I couldn't agree more. And I actually first saw him speak thirty years ago on ancestry and ancestors and have followed him off and on since. He's in a really terrific place with a great message that speaks to what you just said.

Here are some of the things he said in that show: He says that right now there's a battle for the very essence that makes you unique, a battle for your very humanness. He says the capabilities that these technologies appear to give us digitally, we already have all those capabilities in every cell of our bodies. He says that we are the technology, basically, that we need and can grow from.

But I'll back up and give the image that most people may remember from a movie called *The Matrix*: In *The Matrix*, a lead character is off to save another lead character, and she has to fly a helicopter to do so. She doesn't know how to fly a helicopter. So, there's a device inserted into the back of her head, and she downloads the instructions on how to fly this helicopter. In that scene, it's pretty great because she goes off flying the helicopter and saves the gentleman she's supposed to save. That's all very fun in Hollywood, but in another way, it's programming us for what is about to emerge.

Tech companies are developing the very first chip that will be implanted into your brain, and the purpose of this chip is to connect your brain directly to the hard drive of your computer without a cable. This is essentially Bluetooth technology. And with this chip implanted in your brain, you can learn anything — language, math, even how to fly a helicopter. Now, we are being told this is fantastic and we should be embracing this kind of technology, but where is the humanness in this? Where is the love, the compassion, and the understanding? Seems to me it would be pretty easy to get off-track if we follow this path too fully.

THE Z'S:

Again, as we were just saying in the prior answer, we will ask you to find out what is the end goal of the creator of this technology. But also, what are the risks? Where can this technology be turned against humanity, either by one human or a group of humans? And most importantly, the list you just gave is benign — the idea that you as a human could learn math or a language or how to fly a helicopter. Is any of that really relevant? You see, not everyone has access to a helicopter anyway. Helicopters will, in the not-too-distant future, seem like an old relic in terms of Earth's history, and any human being who applies themself can learn more about math or a language. So you see, people are not paying attention to the lack of promise in the promise. And equally they are not paying attention to the lack of heart or asking in what way this is furthering humanity, not just the consciousness of humanity, but the world at large.

You are in a period when certain people in power — who have consolidated and developed their power to such a level — are playing a seduction of power game with people who are still removed from power.

The structure of your Earth has set up a very "us and them" game in terms of resources, in terms of rights. And there are so many power games that you are all constantly asked to play out. Whether it's to do with racism or sexism or transphobia, you are asked to see and feed and be a part of all these different separation games on Earth so that separation remains part of your psyche. And by the way, we are not saying to those of you who are working on behalf of some of those causes that you are doing the wrong job; we are just asking you to look at the bigger picture, energetically. It's always good to zoom out. Even if you are one who is designed to work on the close-up of an area of the world — perhaps it's your job to be an engineer in one of these areas energetically — at the same time, zoom out and see the bigger picture.

This example you just gave is *exactly* what we were discussing in the prior answer, and the questions you have to ask are very important. For human beings must start asking questions, recognizing their compliance, asking where their compliance is coming from, and understanding they have been taught to worship power, money, and those who have all the resources. You have to ask yourself, "Why?" Why are they more worth worshipping than the grandmother who has very little but is helping to raise her grandchildren in the most powerful, heartfelt way because she believes in the goodness of the world? And if you really start to pay attention, you will see these hierarchical structures and recognize how you have been taught to play the game with them. And then you will understand why it is so easy for those with the resources or the power to enact their desires upon everyone else.

DIANNA:

Thank you. There are some very positive implications to some of these technologies. I think of people who've had strokes or suffer from neurological deteriorations (just to name a few) that might benefit a great deal from a modified version of such technology. But I agree, we need the big zoom-out; we need to look at the big picture. And where it really tugs at my heart is with children, teenagers who have grown up with nothing but this technology, these devices in their hands. They don't have the same information or perspective with which to zoom out.

In my personal experience as a fifteen-year-old, that *D* that was on the top of my math exam when it got handed back to me was not for "Dianna." I'd like to think the *D was* for "Dianna," but it wasn't. So, if I were fifteen now and tired of being humiliated for not being very good at math, it would be very tempting if you said, "Oh gee, let us put this device in your brain and hook you up here where you can download everything about algebra or calculus into your brain, and you'll pass the next test with flying colors."

It takes me back to the parenting responsibility you mentioned earlier. I lived in New York City for a long time in the 1980s and 1990s, where it was known at the time that a lot of parents would have their babies on the best kindergarten waiting list before they were even born. There was enormous pressure on parents to push their children to learn, push them to achieve — all to get them into the best schools. The competition was intense.

If we move forward in this way, basically hooking children and teenagers up to download everything they need, then why would they even want to zoom out and see the reasons why this might not be a good idea?

I feel it is very important that we all take some time and zoom out and see the world we're creating for our children and young people. Where's the journey? Where are the challenges in life? Where's the humanness?

THE Z'S:

If ever you want to test what you are saying, Dianna — or any of you who are listening or reading or taking this in — test how willing those in power are to have a zoom-out or to have that alternative conversation. And you will soon notice when they are not willing or when they are censoring or when they are trying to push or force people in a certain direction. That will always be the confirmation that human interests are not what they have at heart.

DIANNA:

So, could we move the discussion to heart, because I said, "Who's in charge?" Is it brain, mind, or heart?

THE Z'S:

Heart.

DIANNA:

There we go! Let's talk about how the heart has that deeper link to the soul, how the heart carries great intuition. Can you share more about the heart with us?

THE Z'S:

Many of you are used to the idea of the sun bringing heat, life, and sustenance to the Earth. Well, in a way, you can see your own heart chakra as the sun inside you. It doesn't mean the sun needs to be shining all the time. Night energy is very important; the energy of the moon is very important. You would not want to be in the sun the whole time. However,

> *your heart is a powerful force.*
> *It is a key to manifestation for many of you.*
> *It is a key to what you attract. It is a key*
> *to how you move through the world.*

For example, those of you who have ever practiced gratitude for any period of time notice your life gets better. And it is not because your life is suddenly protected from all challenges or lessons you have to go through, but because you are learning and practicing being grateful for what *is* there. You start to notice the higher vibrations a little more, and then you start to create them. You start to mirror-create the higher vibrations *outside* you that you are cultivating, generating, and feeding *inside* you.

This is important to understand. When it comes to the heart, the heart is your leadership. It is why so often (you see this in movies and stories), when the heart stops or when the heart ends, the human ends. And as we have told you, the soul and the human are inextricably intertwined in a given lifetime. Now, you are generally not told that. You are supposed to think of the human as a body and that the soul isn't necessarily real. That's very much the programming that has existed for the mainstream.

Your heart is powering the show.
It doesn't mean the heart is superior
or can work in isolation from all the other
parts of you, but it is your sun.

It is the part of you that is guiding you and leading you forward. Approximately fifteen years ago (we are aware you are privy to this, Dianna), we delivered a recording through Lee, and the title we gave was a clue. The title was "Ask the Heart (For It Knows Everything)." It truly does. It doesn't mean it can explain everything to you in words, but it knows everything about your future path, less so your past.

You often think of heartbreak as coming from your heart, but that tends to be the mind replaying past low vibrations. The mind has a direct connection to your emotion. The mind pulls up an emotionally charged memory that creates a lower vibration in your body so that you can play through and clear and heal some of that past energy in your energy field and continue to open to the future. The heart is very much about the future.

Those of you who have been through heartbreak and felt all shut down because you were in heartbreak, have you noticed that you cannot even look at the future when you are in that state? You don't necessarily believe there is a future, and you don't want to know about the future. You are horrified because there is now no future. It is because you are in heart-break. The heart has shut down its light, which means the heart has shut down its future.

And when you go through these heartbreak periods, they are not necessarily the wrong choice. For many of you, it is how you clear ancient grief. Some of it is not even yours; it is ancestral. But it's important to understand and to notice the space you are in. When your heart is closed down, does your mind only tell you a doom-and-gloom story, or is your higher mind allowed to creep in every now and then and remind you not only that "this too shall pass," but that on the other side of this, you are going to open up in a more powerful way?

DIANNA:

To go back to the recording "Ask the Heart (For It Knows Everything)," you have a wonderful quote in there that says something along the lines of: hearts aren't breaking in two; they're breaking open — opening to greater experiences and greater expansion.

THE Z'S:

Yes. And when the heart is going through what you would call a heartbreak period, it is taking time to clear out the old and the dense so that, when that is cleared from the energy field, more life force energy can go toward amplifying the heart for the future.

DIANNA:

And we want to remind people: heart energy is flooding into the Earth. You talk about that in the same recording. And given what you said about Earth being about heart, (for me at least) that's a very positive thing to hear.

THE Z'S:

We'll put it this way to you (and this is perhaps a strange thing for us to say, for there is heart energy in various places, universally): heart energy is *the* most important currency on Earth when it comes to looking at Earth's place in the Universe. Are there other wonderful resources? Yes, but

heart energy is the most important, abundant,
and creational energy on Earth.

That is why there have been limits upon it until this time. That is why there have been those who did not want humans to remember their sovereignty and their heart power. That is why, in a way, the energetic war that you are playing out on Earth right now has long been on the planet, but you are now in a bit of a final battle around it all. Because once humans get back in touch with their heart power, they start to connect more universally.

Think of it this way: you as a human are at your happiest and most fulfilled when you are living your purpose, when you are experiencing a purposeful life, purposeful relationships. And when we say "purposeful," we don't necessarily mean purposeful for other people — that you are achieving all the achievements or doing all the things that are making everyone else happy. No, we mean when you are running your divine energy through you and doing what you are supposed to do. For example, there are *many* on your planet who feel incredibly purposeful around the work that they do or the parenting they are giving. The work they are doing might put them in the bottom (let's say) 10 percent of the planet when it comes to what they earn or the resources they are given for doing that work, but many are also some of the most purposeful, aligned, and happy people on Earth.

Equally, many whose salaries are in the top 10 percent are the most disconnected and detached from their heart. Often they try to keep building more and more and more to try to make themselves happy, rather than recognizing that building something should come as a by-product of purpose and happiness; it is not something you do to try and make yourself happy. And if you are still building the same thing ten years later and you're not happy yet, then you really need to go and have a chat with your therapist because the thing that you are building is not ever going to be the thing that will make you happy. And the fact that you haven't woken up to that is a bit of a shame for you, for there is so much to be found in your sense of purpose.

Imagine the heart energy of human beings allowed to return. Imagine how purposeful humans will become in their role on Earth, but also how much the opening of their heart will connect them to the opening of their spirit and thus spirit beyond.

*Imagine how powerful Earth would become
if it was full of open-hearted, connected
people. And then imagine the effect universally.
Earth has the potential to bring
harmony to the Universe.*

That is the potential for Earth. We're not saying it's the only planet that can do it, but at this moment in time, and for the next three hundred years from when we are making this recording, Earth has the most potential to help the Universe achieve a higher level of harmony.

And the other thing we will say is, Earth is also a place where many of the seeds of disharmony are sewn, which is why the healing of Earth is so important.

DIANNA:

That's beautiful. And I want to end on the notion of oneness again and how we are in a multidimensional Universe. You say there is now more multidimensional assistance than ever. Why is that so?

THE Z'S:

For the exact same reasons that we just told you. Some-times people have an idea that we are benevolent and self-less. For example, there will be those who will thank Lee for what we do or what we bring, but you have to understand, it doesn't work like that. Again, that comes from religious programming and the idea that the savior is higher than you. Look at this "guru trap" that you have on your planet, this ridiculous notion that one human being should be seen as superior to all the others because they are a conduit for a spiritual power that the others are tapping into. By all means, be grateful to that guru, but don't fall into the power games with them and don't dismiss and diminish your own power. Be grateful for them in the same way you would be grateful for someone who gave you something that you were able to recognize was important.

We are not saying that teachers are not required; they are. We see teachers as bridges — bridges to information, bridges to experience, bridges to higher versions of yourself. Lee is a bridge. That is his design, and he bridges in many different ways, in many different aspects of his life. Equally, Lee has found bridges who connect him, and he is very grateful to them. So you see, it should always be a connective web.

*The reason so many multidimensional beings
are working with and interested in Earth
is because Earth is crucial
to Universal harmony at this time.*

And the seeds of war that have been planted and grown on Earth also hold the potential to jeopardize the balance of the Universe. The multidimensional beings are not just here helping you humans; they are here helping the energy of things. And to take it even further, you are not just here as a human, you are not just this human identity — you are an "energy being" who is currently experiencing yourself as human in order to be part of this journey that you are on. And the rebalancing of planet Earth is a huge part of why you are here, even though you may be completely and entirely focused on your own life and the people that you know. But we want to stress, there's nothing wrong with that.

Some of you spend so much time being a humanitarian that you forget to heal your own humanity. And you also tend to revere the people that you think are helping others. But if you look closely at their lives, you will see that some of those who do humanitarian work would become far more powerful if they also did some self-healing; then their humanitarian actions would be even more amplified.

The reason we bring this up — and we have said this all the way through all of our time where Lee is our voice — is that it is so important to understand that one action that you do or one purpose that you are focused on is enough. We have perhaps intimidated or scared some of you with all the information we've given you, and suddenly this idea of your planet or the war energy on your planet has put you into some kind of shock horror. And yet the most effective thing you can do to help all of that is to really get in touch with your own heart, your own love, your own purpose here on Earth. If you do that, you will have an extraordinary effect, not just on your life and the lives of those you are directly in relationship with, but on the planet's vibration as a whole.

This is why we say to you, you are not waking up your minds; you are waking up your heart and your soul. And in order to wake up your heart and soul fully, you need to observe and release the parts of your lower mind, your lower feelings that have been handed to you in order to steer you away from the greater power that you are as an incarnate human soul on this planet. That is why we have been speaking to you so much about the energetics of what we call "the new human soul." We are talking to you about who you are becoming and how you are unbecoming who you were. That is our intent.

DIANNA:

Thank you. I'm left with a feeling of real inspiration to live from my heart, to create from my heart, and not to create from fear.

THE Z'S:

And you, like all reading this, do that very well. Remember the most important thing about this conversation: if you leave this conversation feeling in any way disempowered rather than empowered, look at what were the triggers in the conversation that put you into fear, or concern, or alarm, and really spend some time letting those things open inside you. For example, we have told you about some very ancient agendas that have been at work on Earth. And the way that your minds have been programmed, you can start to get scared about the villain or the group of villains who are here. We do not see it that way. We are not seeing it in a right/wrong way; we are simply telling you what you are overcoming right now, and you can't overcome it unless you see it, unless you acknowledge it.

So, we ask you to not just recoil from some of the things that you notice you are recoiling from, but instead to investigate them, ask questions about them, notice why you're feeling what you're feeling. *That* is the way through those areas in you that would get stuck or shut down. And when you spend a little time doing *that* (and we know that there is going to be time and space for you to do that in the coming weeks and months), then you will be amazed at the life force that reemerges into you as a result of that investigation. Your life force is the gold of your Universe.

Your life force is the gold of your experience
as a human soul on Earth right now.
Let that life force come back to you.

It always wanted to. And now you are at a time in human history when it is going to come back to you at lightning speed compared to any other lifetime you have ever gone through. That, dear friends, is a gift and a joy.

And *that* is why we say to you — despite all that we have said about what you are dealing with, going through, facing — it is a gift and an incredible experience to be incarnate as a human, particularly at this time on Earth.

Good.

In peace and in love to all.

Chapter Three

CONVERSATION SIX

Topics

- The multidimensional nature of the Z's
- How the Z's (and other nonphysical beings) connect with humans
- How best to communicate when we intuitively feel the energy of others
- Wanting to be seen but also fearing being seen
- Social media technology and comparison energy
- Recovering from our "wounding stories"
- Helping empaths balance the energies they receive from others
- What premonitions actually are
- The nature of our intuition

CONVERSATION SIX

DIANNA:

Welcome back to *Conversations with the Z's*. This is conversation six. Welcome, Z's.

THE Z'S:

Good. Welcome. A pleasure to be resuming this dialogue.

DIANNA:

In this conversation, I want to talk more about the word "multidimensional" and how we work with it consciously. We have established that the word "dimension" is a human, third-dimensional term that we are using to try and explain that which would be best explained with higher math — a math that is far greater than any of our human brains could calculate. A challenge for me has been to find ways you (the Z's) and I can dive deeper into explaining how to work with our multidimensionality.

Words are not great teachers in and of themselves, and yet they are the tools we need to use to have these conversations. But experiences and feelings do teach. So, my goal in all our conversations is to use words to create a feeling sense, akin to an experience, that could bring a better opportunity for understanding. So, for the purpose of our conversation today, I would like to discuss "dimensions" from the perspective that they are "states of consciousness."

They are not finite spaces. Instead, they are fluid states of "energy consciousness." Each state of consciousness offers us access to another level of knowledge and wisdom. It also allows for different manifestation possibilities. The attraction, as I feel it, to learning to consciously connect with the vibrationally higher states of consciousness is that they offer the greatest access to what I love to call "the space where all wisdom waits to be invited in." And by "wisdom," I mean our personal, direct, all-knowing connection with creator source energy.

So, how do we help people connect with these multidimensional spaces of knowledge and wisdom? I think we should spiral into that knowledge by talking about some of the styles and ways of communicating multidimensionally. Here on Earth, when we have not seen a friend for a while, we often start our conversations with "How have you been? What have you been up to since the last time we spoke?"

So, out of respect for our limitation of time, I will direct my first few questions just to you, Zachary, and not to all eighty-eight of your group, so that you won't have to give me eighty-eight answers. I will now begin the spiral in.

Zachary, we haven't spoken in over five months. How have you been? What have you been up to?

THE Z'S:

We have been very good. For I am more than one — I am connected to eighty-eight. I am a multidimensional being. So, there have been many experiences, too numerous to recount or track in one or two sentences. That is a human game.

DIANNA:

Can you share what you've been up to?

THE Z'S:

Well, we have been here in the future, as you would experience it. Even today, this act of recording is a future act. Meaning, yes, there is a small number of you humans gathered around electronic devices recording these conversations right now, but in future years and decades to come, there will be many ears, eyes, souls, and hearts engaging with this material. So, for us, it is not so much that we have been doing a great deal in the months since the last conversation; it is more that we have been waiting, watching, and observing you.

What we mean by this is, our sense or notion of time is (as you know) quite different from the human notion of time. You are all experiencing things in a somewhat linear and segmented way. You tend to go from birth to death. You go through a sequence of aging. You go through stages of development, experience, memory, senses, learnings, relationships. For us, we are not playing in such density.

So, if I were to answer your question in a slightly more linear or human way (which we understand is what you want), I would say to you that what I specifically in our group have been doing in the months since we last spoke is crystalline in nature. Meaning, it is without thought, without form, without action even. My experience, as I could best describe it in Earth terms, is that I have been working in the crystalline energy fields around the Earth. My job has simply been to exist in the crystalline space, bringing my energy to it, which both energizes my soul — although I am part of a group soul rather than an individual soul such as the human identity — and feeds the crystalline energy that is now hitting the Earth.

So, it is tricky for us to speak of the things that we do as "separate" or "defined acts," for they are very connected to all of you and what you are doing because you are in relationship with us and calling on us. But we would like to point out that so too does a human respond in the way that is appropriate to the questioner. For example, if a human being asks you what you have been doing these past couple of months, your answer is going to be very different depending on which human being is asking you or which frequency they are open to and holding. This is why you all find people that you connect with, and you tend to stay with them because you want to be able to deliver the most multidimensional answer that you can.

It is not fun or interesting for you to answer that question to someone who is not really interested in the answer but instead is asking you because that is what their programming tells them they *should* do when they first see you after a period of time.

DIANNA:

What is interesting to me about this conversation we're warming up with is that from the dimensional states that you exist

in, *you* have never asked me that question. And I believe —
and I have experienced firsthand — that you already know. So,
my next questions are: How do you know what I've been up
to? Are you reading my mind? And are you accessing my personal auric field? Or are you accessing the Akashic records?

THE Z'S:

This is a very good question, for there is a misconception on
Earth that spirit beings know everything, and that is simply
not true. That comes from your programming around, we
would say, religion or God — that many of you have been
told to believe that there is a higher power that knows far
more than you do. And we would say:

> *higher powers or beings in higher dimensions*
> *know higher information. But that doesn't*
> *mean they are completely aware of everything*
> *that you are going through on a thought basis*
> *or even an emotion or a time basis.*
> *They don't need to be. That is for you.*

What we are aware of is your soul path. For example, in the
past several months since we last spoke, we are aware that
you, Dianna, have been through many different experiences,
which you could give us details about. But what we can see
is the arc of growth — we can see the arc that you have been
through. For example, in your case, you have been through
quite a deepening in the past few months in many different

ways. You could give us the stories of those deepening experiences on a human level, but we do not need them, for they are neither from our viewpoint nor what our relationship with you has to do with.

For example, you have some friends in your life because they are the friends that you laugh with. And you have other friends in your life who are the friends that you have deep conversations or deep learning with. We are not here for the minutiae of human life, for that is not a plane in which we can be of the most assistance. We are here for what you might call the more "broad strokes" of the soul — the destiny themes, the destiny parts of both you the individual and the collective. So, the reason we never ask you what you have been doing is because we know!

Also, we would be talking about events in your history in a way that would imply that they have nothing to do with your present. But your present-moment energy field has everything to do with what you have lived through. So, the truth is, you don't need to know what somebody has been doing in the last twelve months. You simply need to tune in to who they are today.

And if you are aware and awake, as many intuitive souls on the planet are — and indeed, we would argue all humans are intuitive, they just haven't always turned that faculty on yet — in this moment, you could glean what Dianna has been through in twelve months without all the details but by simply sensing the shifts and the changes in her aura. And this goes both ways, for if I haven't seen you for twelve months, you haven't seen me for twelve months either. So I, as the human being who is gazing upon twelve-months-later you, am also different. For no human being goes through stasis in twelve months.

However, there are some periods when you go through great growth in twelve months. And then there are other, quieter, less, shall we say, aggressive developmental phases for the human being. This is why friendships and relationships can go in and out of synchronization. You might be very close to a friend for a decade. And then you go through a period of years, or perhaps the rest of your lives, when you are not as in sync because you have grown or evolved in slightly different directions.

You are all programmed to fear separation or being rejected or abandoned by the group — because you *are* designed to connect, and you have had to do it through very rigid ways thus far — so the loss of friendship can be a fear for many of you. The grief of losing a friendship is not just grief that a friendship has changed or a soul that you had become attached to is clearly going to be someone you are less attached to in the coming months or years. It is also the deep-seated fear in the human being that you will be separate. And that is a spiritual fear.

It is partly human programming that has made you want to gather round and try to force this connection to happen through very human ways. We would say to you:

your true nature as souls is to remember that
you are connected to everything.

But the human game that you have all been born into would seek to tell you a different story.

And that is where the dis-ease — the battle between your soul and your humanity — begins. It is not a battle that you are playing out against yourself or toward yourself. It is a battle that you are playing out that has been, we would say, inflicted upon you in a societal way. And we say that not to scare you or to point the finger at anybody. It simply is a truth. The deep-seated desire to connect and be connected is a soul craving and a soul truth.

However, so many of your human systems and customs have been, we will say, "organized" by your society in ways that don't let you feel as open in your heart or your love or your connection for one another. That is the dis-ease that you are all working through at this time as a society. And you are reaching a boiling point around that, as many of you can attest. For those old rules and regulations are beginning to come apart at the seams.

And while many of you would celebrate this and see this as a wonderful step toward a society of more oneness, the fear that comes up as it starts to break apart is very real for the human body and the human nervous system, which is why these times are tumultuous — transformational, yes, but tumultuous also.

DIANNA:

I want to back up before I ask other questions leading in the direction you were just speaking about. I want to stay a little longer with the notion of how you know things. Because I want to work with teaching myself (and the listeners and readers, if they're interested in this) to use this ability to feel into a person's field — I'm not quite sure what the terminology is, both moving forward and backward in time — as a powerful tool in communication and oneness.

I want to give you an example: You and I spoke about six months ago, and we were talking about some personal things in general in my life. And you mentioned that from the ages of nine to thirteen, I was living in a certain location, and during that time I had to "die" to certain things. That was exactly right. I was nine to thirteen. I have never told Lee about that time in my life, so I can't say, "Oh, you got that information through me talking to Lee." So, how did you know that it was important to share with me? How did you find that information?

THE Z'S:

This may be surprising to some listeners or readers, but we are given the book from your library by your soul in those moments of conversation. There is a perception that perhaps we are somewhat all-knowing or all-seeing and that we have the power to offer you information that is helpful. But you see, that comes from the very human notion that you are separate from spirit. And again, this is how most of you have been raised, so there is nothing wrong with it; there is nothing "less" about it — it is how Earth is constructed right now. And that is why, to many people, the concept of soul communication would not make any sense to them. And that's OK.

But why we bring this up to you is, in that moment of conversation when we were in dialogue with you, soul to soul, we were cocreating with you. Because that is what this conversation is.

This is a soul conversation that you are having with yourself through connecting with us, just as you could connect with other spirit beings in the Universe. It is all available and possible.

There is nothing special about a certain guide or being, even though we understand there are hierarchical ideas about certain angels on Earth. And that is all OK. So, in the moment of reflecting on an area of your personal growth, it was relevant for your soul to hand us a book from your library that explained to us that between the ages of nine and thirteen, you went through several death experiences.

And the reason that we were able to read that book for you was because you gave us permission. Any kind of spirit communication — whether it is this form of channeling or intuition or mediumship or any other term that it is given on Earth — is *always, always* an act of collaboration. It is never a hierarchical act. It is never something that is done to you, the human. It is something you are in relationship with.

The reason that Lee doesn't need to know any of that is because Lee was not there in your history. And even if he was (at that age), it would not necessarily be relevant for him to know all your information. And that is why we say, we do not need to know all your information or your details, for we have the books that contain the themes. And we are here to speak to you on a soul level.

Now, with a traditional Earth-based therapist or counselor, or someone whose work it is to hold space for the stories, experiences, and events in a person's life, it is very good for them to be very involved in your details. For through those details, you are unearthing parts of yourself, healing parts of yourself, refining parts of yourself and your story. But for us, the details are not usually needed for very long because we are always drawing you back to your most expanded self, which lives beyond the details, if that makes sense.

DIANNA:

It does. You and I share the same goal, which is that all these conversations are designed to empower people to learn how to do these things for themselves or to grow an interest in wanting to explore them in the future. So, I really appreciate you saying that this is not about you having all the wisdom and knowledge about me. You're just sharing how I can actually access it for myself, which is where we're headed further into this conversation. But I'm going to stop here and just ask you a little bit about that book —

THE Z'S:

We would like to add one thing before we divert, which relates to an earlier question of yours. In the opening question, you spoke about multidimensionality and the experience of being human. And we would just like to qualify that

the experience of being human is
multidimensional. So, even the most, shall
we say, spiritually skeptical people on Earth,
or those who do not believe in anything to
do with energy or intuition, are having a
multidimensional experience as human beings.

It is just that their minds have been taught to edit it a certain way. For example, you might be born as a free spirit with a free mind, but if you are put into a culture that is quite rigid and asks you to close down in certain ways, you will go in one of two directions: you will either conform over time, or you will rebel, self-destruct, go through all kinds of issues because you are unable to conform.

And of course, later in life you can always open up again. This is why many people have epiphanies in their fifties or sixties, where they realize they are suddenly connecting with their soul or their true essence in a way that they had tamped down for a long time. But the reason we have to give this qualification is, there is sometimes a belief among the spiritual community that multidimensionality is not happening all around you all the time.

And we would like to state that it is. It is just that your minds and your cultural engagement have been trained to not see that. For example, the very reason we started this conversation is because you were asking, "Why do humans ask each other how they are doing, how they have been?" And we would say, in a more multidimensionally aware society, that question would be unnecessary. The person would just stand in front of their friend or the person they haven't seen for a while and would look at them and feel them and take them in for a minute or two. And then they wouldn't need to say, "How are you doing? How have you been?" They would know. They would be sensing and connecting with the person in the now. But you see, because of the separation on this planet, you all need somewhat formal handshakes in order to connect with each other.

You subconsciously ask yourselves, "Is it safe to feel this person's aura? Or perhaps if I give them the code sentences that we've all agreed to first, then they won't feel intimidated when I really take them in with my eyes or my senses." A lot of it is shyness because humans are not used to fully taking each other in with hearts, eyes, senses. And for many, being seen like that can be quite an intimidating moment, for they feel the soul presence of the one taking them in. But they are aware that they have enclosed *their* soul in quite tight clothing.

And so, for the human who is tightly clothed, being gazed upon by one with very open eyes and heart can provoke a certain level of distress. This is why it can sometimes be triggering or too much for certain people to suddenly be confronted by a very open-hearted, open-souled being. It can make them uncomfortable.

And often, those of you who are the open-hearted or open-souled being will misinterpret that and think it's about you. You will say, "Oh, I was too much," or, "Oh, I was a bit too overpowering or a little too intense." No, not at all. You were being you. But for them, that full experience of you that you were bringing only highlighted to this other person (not necessarily mentally consciously, but energetically) how enclosed or shut down they were.

They start to vibrate in an uncomfortable way. As they feel the beam light of your soul looking at them, they start to realize how constricted they feel. And sometimes their mind will blame you. They'll turn it on you and say, "Ugh, I do not like that person. That person is too intense. I don't like the way they look at me." Well, you are just looking at them in an open way. So, we just wanted to qualify that.

DIANNA:

That's an excellent qualification of what we were talking about, because you bring up a couple of things in those comments that I want to address. One is: How do we help people become more comfortable being able to read a field, or share a field (I'm not sure what the terminology is) when someone they are with comes in and they are sensing without words? How do we make that a more comfortable form of communication in people's minds and let them experience or test or try it?

The other is: Of course, under all that is fear, fear of being seen. It's interesting that we live in a culture today where we *so much* want to be seen. You can see it with the likes and the dislikes on all sorts of internet platforms. Yet there is this "see what I want you to see, but don't *really* see me" attitude. That's kind of commingled in there with what you just said, in my opinion.

THE Z'S:

We will start with your first question. Many of you who are reading this have become quite skilled at making it "safe" for other people. And many of you do this as second nature now. You perhaps learned the hard way not to say what you see too quickly. And you have figured out how to make someone comfortable with a handshake before you give them a hug. And by the way, not everybody wants a hug, and that's OK — we would like to qualify that.

For example, let's say you have become quite adept at sensing what is going on for someone. That doesn't mean you know somebody's every thought, but you *can* tell that the person who just walked into the room is feeling a little down or a little sad. You get a feeling that they are carrying something that they just came through.

Perhaps they had a difficult argument with someone. Perhaps someone in their life is dying and they are carrying that around with them. They aren't necessarily speaking about it to people, but you feel it. You can sense it when they come in. So, instead of diving straight into that, you — as a skilled communicator who knows that not everybody wants to go straight for a big "soul hug" — might ask them a question or two to make them more comfortable.

You might say, "It's nice to see you. Can I get you a drink? Shall we sit down?" You, in a way, start the conversation at, let's say, a level one, two, or three, so that they also have time to acclimatize. And this is very important. It is no one human being's job to force open another human being. If you are really coming from a place of harmony and oneness, you will always go at the speed that someone else needs, just as you would like them to do for you when you are in a moment of distress or perhaps needing someone to help you reconnect.

You always want people to be sensitive to the way you are wired. There are some people who like things to be quick and to the point, and they are ready to go there. And there are others who need things to be a little gentler, a little slower. You're all unique in that way. To go back to this friend who has come in and you can sense that they are carrying something, perhaps you gently make them feel comfortable with a few sentences, and you ask them if they would like to go to a different environment.

You start to give them permission to dictate the terms of the meeting, somewhat. And the effort that you are making is to make them more comfortable, whether by offering them a cup of tea or asking, "Would you like to be in a different sitting room?" or even making small talk, just to let them warm up to you and your frequency.

But then, perhaps at a certain point, because they start to feel more comfortable and they have been in your auric field or energy field for longer, they will start to relax and acclimatize. But if you were to, shall we say, just stand there and stare at them for a minute when you could tell they were uncomfortable, and you started saying things like, "My heart can feel that you're distressed," and you noticed that they bristled or tensed up or pulled back, that would be a sign for you to change tack, change direction.

If you truly wanted to support an opening with this person, then you would go a little slower and recognize when they were feeling uncomfortable and work to, perhaps, make them feel a little more comfortable. Equally, if you realized you were not in resonance with this person, this was not your moment with this person, you could choose to end the conversation before anything opened up.

The reason we bring this up is, so many of you remember a time when someone made it safe for you to have what you might call a "spiritual epiphany" about something, or to suddenly realize you were intuitive in certain ways and to not be *scared* of your intuition as so many of you have been taught to be.

Every human being is intuitive.
That is the truth.

It doesn't mean they're all using it, aware of it, or conscious of it. And nor does it have to be that way right now either. For often, there is a superiority in spiritual or intuitive people, in that they think everybody should be at the same level of consciousness. That is not how Earth works right now. That is not what you have come through. But for those of you who are already comfortably seated in the dimensions of spirituality and intuition, so much of your work involves making that more comfortable for others to be in.

Now, we will say something that we have said in the prior conversations in different ways, but this is important:

*It is far less important that you have a
conversation with someone about spiritual
beliefs than it is that you let them be
comfortable in your auric field.*

What we mean by this is: Let's say you have a very skeptical relative or friend, and yet you love them and there is a
connection between the two of you. It is far more important
that you have a harmonious connection with them in a conscious way. You may be recognizing they are uncomfortable
with certain topics or certain areas of discussion, so, be in
your heart with them and make the room comfortable if you
can. But not at your own expense so that you are tolerating
difficult energy from them in order to do this.

Your energy fields are so much more informational than
anything from your mind. You may think you have all kinds
of spiritual information in your mind. And we will say: No,
no, no! Your mind is just interpreting what your energy field
is remembering. So, your energy field is far more interesting
than your human mind, actually.

But the human mind has become the almighty power on
Earth through which you, as humans, are supposed to share
information, which is why you have such an imbalanced society at the moment. All this pressure and all this emphasis
is put on the mind, whereas actually what people truly want
is their hearts. They want to feel comfortable. It doesn't mean
everyone is going to be warm and fuzzy. It doesn't mean everybody is going to demonstrate heart in the same way.

But through the heart, the energy in the center of your chest, you can feel comfortable to be present, can feel a sense of peace in a room, in a relationship, even within a difficult area in your life or a conflict you are having. Can you come back to your heart quickly or consciously when you recognize you have left your heart because you have gone into fear?

That brings us to fear. So, we would ask you to reiterate the fear question to us, please.

DIANNA:

The fear question is about wanting desperately to be seen, which I see in a lot of people in our culture. They want to be seen, appreciated, understood, because so many people don't feel like they are in their lives. But at the same time, they are afraid of what that might look like or feel like: "So, if I have this open heart and you start seeing my open heart…" Many of us are used to knowing that that means we could get hurt.

I think our society has allowed us this interesting place of "create the image you want people to see you as online on the internet or on other platforms," but you're still not really being you: "I'm going to try to create an image of myself that won't be hurt." The image can be created from fear and a need to protect who you really are. And I constantly feel this tug-of-war with people to want to be seen, but then they're not really able to be seen in the way they want to.

THE Z'S:

We very much appreciate this question, for it opens several layers that are important to understand. Firstly, we will say this: We agree with you that many feel they want to be seen or heard. But none of them actually want to be seen or heard. They want to be felt, but they haven't understood this yet. They want to be felt by others. But even more importantly, they want to feel inside themselves.

Many people will go hunting for external validation because they think it will make them feel good. They think it will fill them up. They think the emptiness that they feel inside themselves will be eradicated because enough people will tell them how wonderful they are. And here is the brilliant thing about that: people telling you how wonderful you are will expose all the areas in you that you don't believe are wonderful.

It won't actually make them better. It will make them worse. So,

> *the great gift of being seen and heard is,*
> *it allows you to go one step deeper.*

Once you feel you have been seen or heard enough in your life, or by enough people, then you go after "feeling."

> *You want to feel, and you want to feel*
> *connected to others in your life. You want to*
> *feel connected to yourself. You want to feel*
> *connected to this Earth, including nature.*

That is why nature is so extraordinary for all of you. You all go out into nature. And unless you are completely shut off to what is going on out there — which certainly is the case for many — over time, if you keep putting yourself in nature, your walls will eventually come down. Nature is an alive being. And when you are out there, you feel it. That is why so many say, "Oh, I felt so much better because I took a walk."

Yes, the walk outside definitely did your biology good. For sure, it activated your biology in a very healthy, healing way, and that is one thing. Nature is crystalline, but it is more than just crystalline; it is elemental, it is mineral, it is alive, and it is sensory — there are so many aspects to it we could break down. So,

when you are out in nature, you get to
reconnect with your sensory body.

The reason we took that slight diversion is because everyone wants to feel connected inside themselves. And this need to be seen and heard stems from that. You are also in an early phase where technology is concerned. There is this, shall we say, fascination with the latest shiny object, which compels you to put mirror images of yourself onto the internet that other people will engage with. And they are not (in many cases) mistruths, but they certainly aren't the whole story.

And there are some people who are carefully constructing their image in a few areas and omitting several others. But this is why, for example, your social media (if not used in a healthy way or a conscious way) can be very distressing. Many people feel that they have gotten lost in comparison when they look at all these people online living their fabulous lives, supposedly. Scrolling on social media made them get stuck in comparison. Why? Because the very people posting those pictures have comparison issues in their energy field; otherwise you would never feel it. If you were looking at pictures of genuine joy, genuine connection, number one: you wouldn't have those issues come up in you in quite the same way; and number two: you would get fed by them for a few minutes and then you would move on, and you would want to go and experience the real thing. You wouldn't need to live through a screen to get that. You would want to experience the real thing. So, please understand, we are not in any way being dismissive of those of you who are spending time on the screen.

We say technology is in its infancy because you are in an early stage of technology and the use of it, where many of you are a little dazzled by the whole thing. And that's OK, for you are learning from it. But the most important thing we can convey to you here is, if you are in a room with someone and you feel their energy field, you are perhaps getting twenty-two points of information about that person. For example, there are twenty-two things about that person that you might feel, sense, pick up on. It doesn't mean you interpret them all with your mind. It's not that you would say, "Oh, here are twenty-two things I just learned about my friend who I was in a room with for five minutes." No, you wouldn't necessarily interpret more than six things, most of you. But the information is there in the energy field. A photograph gives you far less.

For example, a photograph might give you three or four points of information about a soul. Now, if you are an intuitive and you are able to use photographs as intuitive mirrors into the soul, that is different. But for most people, they will pick up on what the surface image is trying to project. For example, "Here I am, so happy with my family on holiday. Look at us standing in front of the pool."

But what is far harder to read from a photograph — but it is there — is some of the sadness the person was feeling that day. Your soul would pick up on it if you were in a room with the person, but you get a somewhat distorted view from that photograph. The photograph, if you only look at it in a linear way, is trying to tell you or communicate to you one thing. But if you are an open soul and you look at that photograph, you will feel a little strange, perhaps, intuiting that it isn't "the whole picture."

Again, all human beings — even those who deny that energy exists — are intuitive. So, when you scroll through lots of photographs of people trying to project a happy life, rather than being in a happy life, of course you can feel a bit sad at the end. It is a bit like bingeing on a lot of sugar with no nutrition that gives you an instant feel-good hit. But later down the line, your body goes into all kinds of compensation processes, trying to rebalance you and detox the sugar.

This is why so many of you can get depressed when you look at social media: you are picking up on the inauthentic nature of it. However (and this is important), there are many who are using technology in very powerful, connecting ways. This is the multidimensionality of Earth at work again. You cannot say that something is one thing only. There are so many aspects to it.

Technology has given so many of you a great gift these past twenty, thirty years, for it has connected you more intuitively and informationally. You are a less segregated world in some ways because of your ability to connect with each other, speak to each other about what is going on. That is why there is often a desire to bring censorship to your internet: because that would again put you back into segregation and again control what you're allowed to see and what you're not allowed to see.

We would also like to say that, yes, this technology is in its infancy, and there are many areas that are yet to be fully understood that can have a negative impact on your mental or emotional health, but as with any aspect of life on Earth, the lesson is there. You just have to figure out and move through the stages of growth required to understand what the lesson was teaching you. So, there are many positives.

And there are many who have authentically used technology to facilitate more powerful, honest, and open communication among all of you, and they must also be acknowledged and celebrated. For just as there are a lot of people out there right now using the "mirror effect" to try and create a version of reality that makes them feel good about themselves — and they hope the validation of others praising their world will also make them feel good about themselves — some of that is beginning to wear off, and more and more people are gravitating toward authenticity, sharing, and honesty.

It is also becoming clearer to more people that these are not easy times you are living through. Therefore, many of you can now recognize that a photograph that is all sunny and (if you like) focused on light and love and joy and celebration but doesn't feel authentic is actually as artificial as some of the systems of your world that you are now breaking down and transforming from the inside.

DIANNA:

I appreciate you saying that because I am seeing more people feeling discouraged — or perhaps that word is a little strong — because they create an image on social media and then don't get the healing satisfaction they had hoped for. They put a lot of effort into healing not being seen as a child by wanting to be seen maybe as this adult or older teenager. The initial thrill wears off and then they start feeling the projection toward this image of themselves they have created for the public on social media. And they don't know what to do with the projections coming at them. They get confused or scared by them. I've seen a lot of spiraling in the wrong direction. But exactly as you said, I think people are figuring it out and saying, "Wait a minute, I don't have to pretend to be those things."

It's almost like they're peeling off the projected part of themselves that they inadvertently created, which has started to become a burden — and getting back to a more balanced place. Could you say some words of encouragement to people who are in that place right now, trying to manage the projections and expectations that are not in their highest, best good, coming from anonymous viewers of their material?

THE Z'S:

Beautifully said. And to go back to something you said earlier,

> *those of you who are afraid to open your*
> *hearts to the world or be seen with an open*
> *heart in the world — all of you who have*
> *fear about that — have experienced*
> *negative kickback in a past life.*

So, any of you who have any fear of persecution, judgment, or being rejected or attacked by society because of your open heart, your open mind — you are *all* either working through old imprints from the Earth where that happened to you or you are in an ancestral line where that level of persecution and rejection was strong.

And by the way, that doesn't make you special or unique. If you go back in time a hundred, two hundred, three hundred, four hundred years, life was more brutal in many ways. So, it is quite recently that these memories and these wounds surfaced. Firstly, we need to mention *that*. For one of the issues that many will have about stepping out online is, it means suddenly dealing with an anonymous mass of people, which is very different from what most of you would have experienced, say, fifty years ago when the internet communication web was not available. So, all of you are figuring out how to keep yourself balanced — psychically, emotionally, mentally, energetically — when you put yourself out there into that wide, open playing field.

Secondly, what you said about children who weren't seen or heard, who are now in adult form trying to heal or process that wound by putting themselves out there, we do need to remind everybody that this is a collective experience.

One of the tricky stages for someone going through a healing of something very traumatic that happened to them in their life is the overpersonalization of what they experienced. For example, let's say you were deeply bullied as a child, and you perhaps push this down, try to forget it ever happened, try to erase it from your mind. Then, in your early twenties, a series of events causes you to remember everything that happened, and a few things in your life are going wrong. A friend suggests you go and get some therapy, for example, or start reading a certain book that will open your eyes to how some of what happened to you as a child is now playing out in the behaviors and the experiences in your life. These experiences are asking you to go back and heal your childhood trauma, to go back and love that child inside you who was so deeply wounded by what happened but needed to cover up that part of themselves in order to survive.

Nothing wrong with that, because that is the way that you are all taught to behave — cover it up and move on. But sometimes what you have covered up starts to invade your life. When what you have covered up is taking up so much space in your energy field that it is stopping your progress, your abundance, your empowerment, your next levels of living and learning, you will have to go back and help to heal that part of yourself. So, the personalization is important.

There is a time and a place in your life for you to place your focus on what happened to you and how difficult it was. And that is very important to understand, especially for those of you who have learned to rationalize away what happened to you. It is quite common for many who are sensitive or open to qualify what happened to them, saying, "It was bad, yes, but there are so many other people in the world right now who are suffering more than I am. So, I will just bypass what happened to me because my empathy is drawing my attention to all those other souls who are also suffering, but in a bigger way."

We will tell you that you can give yourself permission to acknowledge that it doesn't have to be one or the other — you can see all these other souls who are suffering and still go back and tend to some of your own, and you will shift your focus as each day goes by. That is the multidimensional nature of life.

You are tending to your own suffering,
and you are aware of and trying to serve or
help or assist with the suffering of others.
That is multidimensionality.

Why we are drawing attention to this "personalization phase" is, during your personalization phase, you might go deeply into what happened to you. But at a certain point, you come to wonder: If this happened to you, what else is happening to everyone else on the planet?

Their story might not be the same. They may not have been brutally bullied in the playground, but they may have been subtly bullied verbally in their family. Not everyone is going to have a bullying story, but everyone is going to have what we will call a "wounding story," a place where they felt wounded as a human being. And many of you have many places and times where this happened to you.

For those of you who are overpersonalizing the fact that you weren't seen and heard, and you're trying to get that void filled, it would be very good to remember that there are many in the world today who are feeling the exact same way or worse than you are in this moment. So, you are not alone. And you are dealing with a collective wound as much as a personal one.

This is why we always say, it is actually helpful to admit to yourself that there are a great deal of wounds on this planet. For some of you, that can be depressing, especially those of you who are angelically wired. You prefer the lighter, brighter side of life, and that is part of your wiring. So we aren't saying you should fixate on this depressing fact that everybody has wounds. But we think that the denial of this truth has not served any of you.

There are many of you who are asked to stay silent about what has been painful or what has been difficult. And that goes back to your earlier question, Dianna, where we were explaining some of the positive sides of your technology in recent years. It is actually beginning to give a space for healing and a voice for healing in ways that are quite mature.

The reason we bring this up is,

the personal wound is always collective.

And while we understand that it will not always serve you to look at it that way — particularly if you are at a very specific stage of your healing journey — ultimately, that is where you will get to. The biggest trick that was played upon you as humans was to isolate you away in your own minds. And also invoking shame — telling you what you should be ashamed of in your thoughts, what you should be ashamed of in your feelings, what personal truth you would be rejected for by society if you ever revealed it to them. That is how you all became imprisoned in yourselves away from one another, and yet your hunger and your desire is to connect with one another. Sure, not all the time — some of you are going to need time alone — but at a deep, intrinsic level, you all know that you are connected and you are the same in essence. And yet you are living in a world that has given you hierarchies around race, around gender, around class, around money — a great deal of illusions that you are all living in as a construct.

So, the threat of separation is constantly around you. Constructs on Earth are constantly telling you that you are separate from each other. And that creates a fear and an anxiety inside you because it is not coming from love. You often hear, "There is only love and fear," and this encapsulates the polarities that you are pulled between on Earth. You all prefer the feeling of love because love is where connection and oneness and spirit exist. Fear is very much a human construct. And fear is present when disconnection is present.

When you are not connected to spirit, your heart, your higher power, and the greater view of what is going on, on your planet and in your life, you will be more in fear. And by the way, don't chastise yourself if this is your truth, for fear is part of the human game and part of the human healing on Earth. And you know that before you sign up to come here. There are some of you who come here to move beyond fear as fast as possible and to become an emblem and a vessel of love and an example for others through that love.

And there are others among you who come here for other reasons. And you are going to go through the gamut of fear and love many times in order to be of service to others from that perspective. So, there is no "better"; we are just giving you the map. And again, we would like to end this answer by reminding you that

> *the world is wounded, but that doesn't*
> *mean it isn't full of light. It is full*
> *of light and consciousness.*

But it is also full of wounds. And if you start to see that clearly, it can empower you to have an easier life, rather than a harder life. But we do understand there is a level of depression or grief or resistance to understanding that the wounds exist all around you, as much as the spirit and the light do.

DIANNA:

I appreciate how much was included in that answer you just gave. But I'm going to go back to the stream of thought about how we communicate consciously, multidimensionally — understanding that we're doing it all the time, whether we're aware of it or not — and some of the ways it may show up in people's lives so they can start to identify what we're talking about more and use it or not use it.

And when I said, "manage the projections and expectations," in my last question, what was coming to mind for me is being told as a young child that I was a "psychic sponge." I'd never heard of that term at the time. It was the 1970s when someone said that to me. I was having trouble understanding how I could cheerfully go into the supermarket, buy what I needed, smile at people, chat with people, chat with the checkout person, leave the store, and have a heavy heart. And that's just a very small example.

I could do it at school. I could do it coming home, picking up something in the family, until one day someone said to me, "Well, you're a psychic sponge!" And it made sense. So, that's the way I would say I was connecting with people's fields — auric fields or energy fields. In retrospect, it was not serving me. And of course, in my case at the time, it was unconscious. I just noticed the emotional shift in me and wondered what had happened.

Let's start with your perspective on helping people identify that dynamic more and maybe ways they can shift it to becoming an empowered skill and not a detrimental one.

THE Z'S:

Firstly, this is a good focus area for the path for many "psychic sponges." You could also call them "empaths" — there are many different labels and words that can help you identify these patterns of behavior and energetics inside you.

Those who are wired that way tend to go through all kinds of opportunities to learn. And the question is whether or not they *will* learn.

For example, in your case, because you know this about yourself now, you will choose when and if you can go to a certain place. For example, if you are slightly lower in energy, you will decide not to go to the grocery store that day, for you do not necessarily feel strong enough to do it. And you will do it the next day or the day after when you are a little more robust.

There is also a series of techniques that you can all employ. For some of you, words work well. For example, we gave the reciting of this sentence of affirmation to Lee and a workshop room many, many years ago: "I release any energies and emotions that are not mine." This is a sentence that Lee utters repetitively before and after doing any work in which he is aware that he is interacting with the energy fields of many others in a conscious way. He uses it like a verbal mantra. And that is very helpful for him, and for many others who have used it over the years. You can also add a few different techniques. You might visualize yourself in white light. You may play a certain piece of music to yourself before and after. These are ways to clear your field.

But then, there are also choices you can make to draw your energy in. And this is something the empath tends to resist. For example, if you usually walk through the grocery store smiling at people and looking at people, but you recognize you're at a low ebb that day, before you go into the grocery store, you may say, "I'm going to keep myself contained today. I am not going to send smiles out to people because that doesn't quite feel right. And I'm not sure I am in the space to connect with people in that way. I am going to go in and collect the few things I need, and then I'm going to leave. I will be perfectly pleasant, I will be peaceful, but I will not be looking to overly engage. I will not be looking to, perhaps, lose energy through connecting with others and then come out of the grocery store with all kinds of fragments of their energy field now in mine."

If you don't set that boundary, your trip to the store might go more like this, for example: "The woman I smiled at who was deeply sad, a little bit of her sadness connected with me when I smiled at her. And I was unaware of this, and I carried on around the store. And with each person I interacted with or smiled a big, bright, light smile to, I started to collect things from them. And by the time I left the store, I was full of everything inside me that I had touched on in them." Does this mean you had cleared it, healed them, taken it away from them? Not always, and this is a misbelief that some get into (though not necessarily you, Dianna).

They get caught in this idea that they are going into a grocery store and healing everybody. But if they come out feeling quite sick, then nothing was transmuted. In fact, what they were being given was a boundary lesson. They were being shown, "Ah, I need to be a little more mindful of the way I use my energy in here. And I need to be a little mindful of looking after myself and my energy field before I go in and when I come out."

Because, and here is the point, you would have quite a different experience doing the same behavior — walking around smiling, feeling quite light, connecting with people — if you went to, let's say, a festival that was all about love or dancing or celebration, where others were doing that too. It wouldn't be you doing all the giving or doing all the sending of light. You would be in a relay of that with other people. This is why so many of you enjoy dance parties or festivals or places where everyone raises their frequency together. And then you share in that energy. It's how you become quite euphoric and quite "high" together.

But in contrast, if you go into a grocery store where the norm is to be shut down and you don't have excess energy to spare that day or you haven't made it your mission to go in and love everybody,

> *the most important thing to remember*
> *is that learning your boundaries for*
> *your own energy field is crucial for*
> *your impact and your power on Earth.*

This is why we often say that simply striving to be as open as possible isn't the best way of being. Now, you could argue with what we just said, and you could say, "Well, surely, that is a wonderful aim." And we would say: Yes, but you don't get there by only being the most open person possible all the time, because then you won't know how to refine your own energy field.

So, what many of you need to learn to do is figure out who you are inside. Many of you have been taught to identify who you are and how you engage through your *external* relationships. And very few of you were ever encouraged to figure out who you are *inside*. Who are you at the soul level? What's going on inside you? And guess what? You are the *only* person who is ever going to know what's going on inside you!

Even your most beloved friend or partner or the best psychic in the world is not going to know everything that's going on inside you. But *you* are if you pay attention. Many of you have been encouraged to focus outward, rather than inward. And yet,

this is a time in history when more of you
are beginning to understand that if you take
care of your inner world as much as you attend
to your outer world, you will become quite
strong, robust, and balanced.

Dianna, we will come back to you as an example, for the example you gave is very, very common. You have learned that you can be open and generate great love, compassion, and wisdom for others, provided you pay attention to what's going on in *you* that day. So, you now can go to the grocery store in a myriad of ways. You know how to go to the grocery store and be somewhat invisible. You know how to go to the grocery store and give out some excess love and energy because you have it to spare, and it doesn't cost you to do so. You also know how to go there and be a little more "in the middle," a little guarded, not unfriendly, but you aren't going to lose too much energy because you are conscious of the energy you are going in there with and how much you have.

The reason we bring all this up is, so many of you will fall at the first hurdle. You will say, "I'm empathic. I feel everything. I'm doomed." And we would say: You are not doomed. You simply have to learn some things. And you have to learn what affects you and why, and how to find tools and ways to deal with it. But this is very important: For those of you who feel you are, we will say, an "electrical nerve" when it comes to your empathy, for those of you who will say, "I have no filter, I have no boundary," we would say to you: Why? What happened to you in your life so far that you believe you are not allowed to own your interior? Why did you abandon your inner self? Who taught you to do that? Who denied you your own boundaries, your own rules and regulations?

And often those of you who are experiencing that as your story will find that either you were energetically, emotionally, psychologically, or physically violated in your earlier years, or you were born into a group or were in scenarios where you were disempowered by others. And so, the wound of that disempowerment is now all that will talk to you when you are trying to learn about boundaries, learn about who you are and how to look after yourself.

But instead, what often happens is, you are caught up in the emotions of others because either you escape out of your inner body or you were never allowed to go there in the first place. You were always told to be in service or hypervigilance to the emotions, needs, wants, and desires of others. So, if you think you are doomed, we will say: No, you are not doomed, but you are dealing with a wound that you haven't yet fully uncovered. You are dealing with wounds from your past that need a little more care, attention, and work to get to the heart of, so that you can free yourself from past ways of being and move into new ways of being as an empowered, empathic being.

And there is sometimes the separation myth when it comes to the sensitive soul or the empath: "Oh, I am the most sensitive in my family. I am the most empathic in my group of friends." And we would say: OK, well, if you are happy with that role, good, stay there. But if that bothers you, go and find some other sensitive souls and empaths to be around and see how you do, for none of you are separate.

And even those of you who walk around that grocery store thinking you are the most open, sensitive being in there, we would say you are simply displaying it more. And we don't mean inauthentically displaying it — perhaps displaying it to yourself as much as others, tapping into your awareness of how you are feeling — but every other being in there has the same capacity. They just, for whatever reason, haven't opened. And this will amuse you somewhat: the reason you're not spotting the other sensitives in there is because they have learned to draw themselves in in that environment so successfully that you can't even sense them. Ha!

DIANNA:

I appreciate you talking about ways to manage those feelings we pick up and how to be aware of when we want to be that open and when not; and ways to protect ourselves when we're not in the right place to be the beam of light we may want to be that day. Another area that I think gets confusing for people, and maybe more so for empaths, is the notion of premonition.

It's this middle ground between intuition and full-on psychic knowledge.

A lot of people say, "I had a premonition, I had a premonition." And often, the premonitions are negative and fear-based. Sometimes not. Sometimes it's, "I know the phone is going to ring, and oh! It does." Or, "I know someone is going to stop by. Oh! They do." But often, it's a fear-based experience. Could you talk about what a premonition actually is? And how does it fit in with this psychic-sponge, empath energy, if at all?

THE Z'S:

We appreciate this question because the difference between what is fear-based and non-fear-based depends on the individual and the history. For example, let's say you have a premonition of something to come — you suddenly have a premonition that six months from now, you will be alone in your house and aware that, let's say, your partner or your family member who lives with you is not there.

And in this premonition, it's very clear to you that you are alone. It is not that your loved one has just popped out; it is that they are not there in the house anymore. Your human mind and fear immediately start to panic about this because you interpret the worst-case scenario. And perhaps, in your history in this life, you have lost a loved one and that is a fear of yours.

But the fear of losing a loved one is so common on Earth because so many of you have been incarnate here several times and have all experienced losing loved ones or children or parents. So, this comes up a great deal in the subconscious of the human. This premonition may have nothing to do with your worst fear that this person dies or is suddenly not on the planet.

Perhaps your premonition is accurate, but you are merely being shown a time six to twelve months from now when (for whatever reason) this beloved of yours who you normally live with is not going to be in the house for three weeks because of an opportunity that comes their way that takes them away for travel, and you decide you aren't going to go. But in the moment of the premonition, your fear and your thoughts grab hold of it and start to interpret it based on the worst-case scenario.

This is why premonitions are tricky. You can be shown a vision that you interpret six different ways. The vision might be showing you a fact. And your feelings and your thoughts about that vision immediately decide what that fact means, when actually, as we just showed in this example, it could be something quite different. The premonition of being alone in the house comes along, and you immediately panic that your loved one or your child is going to die and is going to be taken from you.

But actually the premonition was simply showing you a period of time up ahead so that you could get used to the idea that you're going to be alone in the house for a few weeks because your beloved is going away and is going to have an opportunity. So, you see, this is where intuition and psychic phenomena can be tricky for all of you, for you need to be very "clean" when you come to those. You need to be able to hold a wide sense of possibility with all visions or intuitions that you have.

We will say that

not all empaths are intuitive. In fact,
the empath who is, shall we say, somewhat
plagued by their level of empathy can have
a great difficulty getting in touch
with their own personal intuition.

If you are one who is overwhelmed by the emotions of others, you are going to struggle to tap into your own higher mind, your own higher visionary mind; it will be hard for you to do that.

There are those empaths who can't help but let the emotions of others dominate their experience. When they walk into a room, they immediately abandon or forget themselves and are so focused on the other three people in the room that they also open an intuitive field for them and start getting information for and about them.

If you identify as an empath and you identify as intuitive, you will know that you are in a good balance with it if you can say, "I am good with my own emotions and know how to regulate them when needed. And I am good with intuitions for myself about my own life and am able to use and work with the intuition I get about myself."

The opposite of this would be, "I am always receiving messages only for other people, and I am easily overwhelmed by the emotions of others." If the latter sentences are your dominant experience, then you know you need to do more work on getting in touch with your inner self and your energetic boundaries.

And as we suggested earlier, there are all kinds of reasons that you abandon your inner self. You do it because you were never allowed to go there. You were discouraged. You were put in a subservient or codependent role when you were young. It wasn't safe. You, perhaps, were highly psychic as a child, and you had to pull out of that at a certain point to be safe in or survive the family unit, which would never have allowed that part of you to be present in any way that would have been good for you.

There are all kinds of reasons that you may abandon your inner self. Premonitions and empathy do not always go hand in hand. But it is very good that you bring up the fear aspect. For the test for all of you, whenever you are thinking about a vision that has, let's say, upset you or given you fear, is to ask yourself, "In this moment, is this true?"

For example, let's say you are stressing for days or weeks about the fear that your loved one is going to die at some point. We would say: Stop. Take a breath. Your loved one is going to die at some point. They might die before you. They might die after you. That is a given, for all of you will die from these human bodies. So, is your fear rational? Is your fear helping you? And this is how you can be mindful around any premonition or vision.

There are two aspects to it. One is the vision or the premonition itself. And that should be something you can fairly logically write down on a piece of paper, such as: "In the premonition, I saw I was alone in the house six months from now, and my partner wasn't here." That is what the premonition told you. Then, the second aspect is how your emotions started to interpret it.

And sometimes you are given a premonition that will start a healing cycle in your body in advance. For example, if that fear of losing your partner is so strong in you that it brings up abandonment or past-life loss, then even if it turns out that they are only going away for a few weeks in six months, for a trip perhaps, the premonition came to prepare you. You may have interpreted this as the loss or death of your partner, but that is not what was being shown. The premonition came to get you used to the idea of being alone for a time, and that it isn't the end of your world. It is just a new phase of experience for you.

So, that is how we would convey what we see, experience, and know in regard to that question, Dianna. But we are happy to elaborate more if you need more specifics in any other areas.

DIANNA:

I think we will elaborate more when we get into our discussions on death, dying, and reincarnation. And by that, I mean, there are people who have premonitions that someone is going to die, and they do. I want to save that for when we get into the realms and planes and discussions around death, dying, and reincarnation.

We've touched on intuitive feelings and intuition over and over again, so I would like to end today with asking you this last question: Intuiting what? And where are we intuiting it from?

THE Z'S:

In much the same way that we do not exist in linear time the way that humans experience it, neither do you.

You are all existing in the past, the present, and the future simultaneously.

But you are *most* focused on the past. Most human beings are focused more on the past than the present, and that's OK. It is not wrong.

It may sound wrong to some of you, but it is actually simply where the timeline focuses for humanity at the moment. You are perhaps 60 percent past and 40 percent present, most of you. And some of you who are futurists, you are often 10 to 20 percent in the future too. So, all of you are existing in the past and the present and the future, but the consciousness of humanity at this time is mostly focused on the present and the past.

In future decades and centuries, the consciousness will align more between present and future. The current sway toward the past will start to shift a touch more toward the future with a bit more grounding in the present for everyone. So, when you ask, "Where do these premonitions come from?" or, "How are you involved in the intuitive realm?" one way we could describe it is, you are all intuitive through your senses.

Often, there is an idea that intuition is simply about the third eye or psychic information or visions. But actually, your intuitive faculty comes through your senses. So, many of you can *feel* that another human being you are standing with is nervous. You might tell yourself through your mind that you worked out they were nervous because you saw their lip quivering and because you saw their body shaking a little bit, and because they didn't seem as calm as they normally do. And for some people, that *is* how they work out that other people are nervous.

But most of you engaging with this material, you will *feel* it. Your feeling, your senses will intuitively understand what is going on. You will read the energy field of that other person before or simultaneously with seeing the symbols, the signs, the indicators that they are nervous. So, when you tap into what you might call your "intuition," where your higher mind or your visionary third eye is concerned, you are simply tapping into the future.

So yes, there are some who get premonitions about people dying. There are some who get premonitions about events that do come true. But other premonitions come along that either change in the timeline or were designed to help shift something for you so that that outcome doesn't need to come true.

Intuition, as we perceive it, and from your perspective, is actually an all-feeling, all-knowing energy that you have inside you,

which is not just about psychic information or psychic visions that get sent your way.

You can all tap into the future at any time if you choose to. If the consciousness shifts enough on the planet, more people will be able to feel comfortable with allowing their intuition to be part of their life. Not all of their life — no one would want to walk around living purely from intuition, for there is far more to your world and your humanity and your soul than that. But you can all tap into the future. Because your future, in terms of the themes of your life, is there from your birth. It is in place.

This is why so many of you have these premonitions about your lives. This happens especially with children — children who are still quite connected to the soul realms. They know what they're going to do, who they're here to be, what they're here for. Not every child has that. But when you pay close attention, you'll see that many children — especially in that first six to seven years for most of them — will tell you a great deal about why they are here, what they have come for.

They can't fully make sense of it with their linear minds, but they simply know it. They know why they came. They know which relationships they came for. They know what they came to do on the planet this time around. They are feeling the future not because they are placing themselves somewhere else in order to do so or are having some extraordinary vision sent to their mind. They can feel it because they are connected to it.

You are all deeply connected to your future.
And the idea that you are not can get in the
way of your manifesting and your abundance.

That is why so many of you will let the past get in the way of what you create. Remember, we said most of you are focused on the past. So, if you were talking to someone who had just come out of a deeply unhappy relationship — perhaps they had lost all their belongings, their home, their money, and they were very much in the wound of that — and you said to them, "I can feel that you are going to have a wonderful future. I can feel that you are going to have a wonderful relationship ahead. You are going to build a beautiful life for yourself. You're going to have the resources you need to do and create what you want to create on this Earth," they would hear you in one of two ways: If they were in the light and the truth of their soul and they could join you in that seeing, they would say, "Ah, yes, that feels good to me." And they may not be able to stay there the whole time. But in that moment, they would feel the truth of it, and it would sustain them long enough to continue to clear out the wounds of the past relationship. But *most* would fight you. Most would be consumed by the wound of the past and what they just went through, and they would not be able to feel the future when you presented that to them. They would start to object, and they would say, "Oh, I don't deserve a good relationship," because that belief would still be in their system.

That is partly what this last relationship affirmed to them, that they don't deserve a good relationship. They would tell you that it's impossible for them to find a house at the budget they've got now because again, they're stuck in the budget they've got now. They're not considering that they could actually increase their finances in the future. So, this is why we say,

developing intuition in your world is key to a better world for all, not just the individual.

When you eradicate the education, awareness, and celebration of intuition, you limit human possibility in the future. And this is something that many are struggling with at this time on Earth. You are seeing the destruction and, in some cases, the manipulation and control of the Earth. And many of you believe you are doomed to that future because you have forgotten that you can build and create differently, and that is part of the power of the soul on Earth.

But because the soul has been, shall we say, removed from the conversation of humanity over and over again, people forget. People forget what they are connected to. It's a creational power that runs through you. So, that is why we give this example of the friend that you are trying to encourage. They are locked into their idea of what they have just been through. And they cannot see that they could build something different in the future because they are caught somewhere between the past and the present.

And by 2050, humanity will get to a point where you are all more firmly in the present than ever before, which will allow the future to come forward in a big way.

DIANNA:

Thank you. I can feel we have more wonderful conversations yet to come. Thank you, Z's.

THE Z'S:

A pleasure. Thank you.

Chapter Four

CONVERSATION SEVEN

Topics

- The Z's "language" and how they communicate through Lee
- The power of symbols
- The experience of exit points
- How we receive psychic messages for others
- The rise of intuition and consciousness on the planet now
- The beauty and power of grief

CONVERSATION SEVEN

DIANNA:

Welcome back to *Conversations with the Z's*. This is conversation seven. Welcome, Z's.

THE Z'S:

Good. Welcome.

DIANNA:

In our last conversation, we were talking about multidimensional communication and different ways we do that. I wanted to ask you to continue with that subject, starting with talking about the Z's. You have said that some of the Z's are not verbal. Can you explain how they communicate?

THE Z'S:

Well, firstly, we must reiterate that we are verbal through Lee in the way that we are because of translation. For example, we do not use this English language that is being used now. Our communication and related roles are similar to how you humans have many different languages, and some among you can speak several languages. You are able to communicate with people from different places in ways that other people are not; they are confined to one verbal language.

In our grouping, there are those of us who are adept at communication through language and translation. Then, there are others in our group who hold different positions, much in the same way that if you meet a group of humans who are either a family or, let's say, a group gathered around a similar work focus, they will all have different skills; there will be one who is a good communicator and very good at bridging the public to the group, and then there will be one who is, perhaps, quiet verbally but highly efficient at getting important work done that the group needs.

All roles are different within our grouping, but we would say of the eighty-eight who are the main formation of our group, approximately thirty-three are proficient with language or are verbal enough to be able to relate information via words. Because often, what you are hearing when Lee is channeling us is perhaps fourth-hand translation. Meaning, the final words that come through his mouth and body are words that I am, shall we say, signing off on as Zachary, for I am the lead spokesperson for the group. However, ten or twelve of us may have handed the words along. And this all happens very fast. It sounds like quite an arduous process, but it is all happening in a split second.

Then the other side of it is, only certain words are allowed. We are not able to simply send words through Lee's body without any consideration of how they will impact all of you. As we are about to utter the words, sometimes at the last minute, a word needs to be changed or the direction of a sentence needs to be diverted because we can only bring into the energy field of the listener that which will be received in a positive way. Meaning, if any word or sentence that we were about to bring through was going to in any way limit or diminish or lower the vibration of the listener or the reader, it has to be adjusted at the last minute.

But sometimes it is only our interaction with the delivery into your energy field that gives us this information. For example, the twelve of us who may have formed the sentences in response to your questioning, Dianna, may have lined up what we feel is vibrationally the perfect answer in this moment for your question. But just as the words are about to go into audible form through Lee's vocal cords and come through his mouth, *that* is the moment when we feel a friction or a tension in the air. And sometimes, words or sentences have to be changed midflow. That is how the "stumbling effect" you will sometimes hear happens.

DIANNA:

That's very interesting. Thank you for explaining that. I want to talk about a symbol I have here on a piece of paper in front of me. I purposely didn't show it to Lee because I didn't want to know that you saw it through Lee's eyes. But using the different ways you communicate and some we've talked about, maybe some we haven't, how can I convey this image to you so we can talk about it? Do you look through *my* eyes at it? Do you *feel* the picture, or should I describe it to you?

THE Z'S:

Well, what we can tell you about this symbol is, it is a heart chakra symbol for you. It activates and opens and expands your heart. That is what its purpose is. We can feel *that* through reading your energy field. But by all means, describe it however you wish to.

DIANNA:

I'm looking at the infinity symbol, as it's called. It's the figure eight, sideways (if you want to look at it that way), and the lines intersect in the middle. I have a question: We call that the infinity symbol. Infinity is not a number — it's a concept of something that is unlimited. How do you experience this symbol?

THE Z'S:

Well firstly, we do not want to disagree with your way of seeing it, for infinity is how it is known. But we see it as "unity," which, of course, is really the same thing. This is why it provokes a heart response in one such as you. For this is a symbol that you have worked with across many, many, many, many, many centuries. You have a lineage that in many ways helped to conceive of some of these symbols, and you were deeply connected (as were many) to the origins of the creation of some of these symbols.

Then, over time, some of these symbols have been altered, but the original imprint remains the same. We will give you an example. At this time on Earth, a very popular pastime is musical artists creating what you would call "cover songs" of previously written songs. For example, let's say eight different singers or musicians or bands have covered the same song.

The essence of the song remains, even though each inter-
pretation may expose or enhance a certain slant of that material, but the one who wrote the original song, *always* their
imprint is felt through any cover version, even if it is quite
concealed and looks and sounds somewhat different from
their original version.

The imprint of what they encapsulated and encoded into
that song is there. It is the same with the symbols. For you
specifically, Dianna, the heart chakra activates with this
symbol because you understand that this symbol was created to remind everyone of the unity of all things, which you
can also translate as "infinity."

We will also say that it is time for some new symbols to appear on Earth. As wonderful as it is to play with the old form
of existing symbols, it is time for more symbols to appear to
represent the new layers of consciousness that are present
on the planet now.

Symbols do not work for everybody, but for those who are
visually sensory, the symbols can impart a great deal of information. However, it's usually memory-based information — so, from the past. This is why we say new symbols
will be a wonderful thing to support what we were speaking
of earlier: a world in which you are beginning to approach
living in the present more than the past — which has not
been your way for a very long time.

Many who are listening to or reading this will also play
with symbology. Many symbols from other dimensions and
other star systems are beginning to hit the Earth in a bigger

way. When we say "hit," we mean appear or manifest on the Earth.

So, this is another aspect of, if you like, the "channeling-of-symbols" world that is going to continue to expand in the coming years. You are going to see more people bringing through symbols that help people remember other lifetimes, other dimensions that, until now, have been, shall we say, removed from Earth's history. But they are symbols that many of you will remember, just like a language that you hear that you don't logically understand but some part of your body remembers it.

Many of you have this with past lives. You may visit a certain country and, for some reason unbeknownst to you, you feel familiar with the culture, with the people, with the places. You can't quite put your finger on it, but you are more familiar with this place than you are with lots of others that you visit. It will be the same with these symbols. There are symbols that are going to appear on and come to the Earth that are going to be a lot more, shall we say, "remembered" in the years to come.

DIANNA:

Is there any correlation between that and what are called "crop circles"?

THE Z'S:

Ha! That we cannot speak of at this moment, for we would go off on a diversion that truly belongs in the conversation on galactic history.

DIANNA:

All right. I'll save that for that conversation. I wanted to talk a little bit more about symbols because you and I had spoken before that —

THE Z'S:

We have to say this now because you brought it up...

DIANNA:

Yes.

THE Z'S:

Harmony is what those symbols in crop circles represent. And harmonization is the aim with, we will say, 95 percent of the crop circles that you see. For many of you, when you look upon the symbols in crop circles, you will feel, sense, or recognize a harmony. What we will tell you is, the symbol in the crop circle is far more complicated than what many of you are used to seeing on Earth. But the reason it is powerful for you is because you realize you understand that complication. You're just not used to seeing it.

The symbols are complex; there are details, layers, and information in those symbols that many of you recognize. So, it is mystifying to you, and you wonder, "Where did these come from, and why did they appear?" But also mystifying is the harmonization of those symbols. Those symbols are most often spelling out "peace" in different ways. And they are spelling it out as a directive and a reminder.

DIANNA:

When I look at them, I also feel they're mathematical equations of some kind. Is there any truth to that?

THE Z'S:

Well, everything is a mathematical equation. For example, in an earlier conversation we spoke to you about the number sequences that music relies on to build itself. Everything can be broken down into number sequences. And part of why your mathematical awareness gets activated when you see those symbols in crop circles is because there are some very complex ideas, symbols, notions in your Earth history that are "truth" for all of you as humans but have been somewhat whitewashed or edited out.

So, when you see a symbol like that, the mathematical complexity of the symbol reawakens you. You recognize it because you *know* it, but you don't understand why, since it is something you have rarely seen and mystery surrounds why and how it appeared. There is still secrecy around these crop circles as spoken by leadership on this planet. And yet the leadership knows exactly what those crop circles are. They have just been, shall we say, forbidden to speak about it to the people.

You are coming into an era when things like this will become a lot more normal, understood, and known to you all. For the impact of those symbols in the crop circles is undeniable to the human body and the human eye.

This is where skepticism comes into play on Earth. Skepticism is a form of what you might call "mind control." You are skeptical of something your mind doesn't understand or has no past frame of reference for (or so it believes). But truth, to a human, is felt. The person who picks up their newborn baby in their arms does not have a logical response. They do not, in their mind only, look at this baby and congratulate themselves for holding a baby that they had a part in helping bring to the Earth. They have a powerful, visceral, sensory experience.

For as they hold this newborn, a couple of things happen: They are taken back to the moment when *they* entered the world, but they did not have the consciousness then that they do as they are holding this new, beautiful being who has entered the world. They are also seeing their own connective thread to creating a new being on Earth, their ability to help seed the biological form of a new soul on Earth.

This is what we mean:

All human beings bypass mental skepticism
when they feel something in their body
that is undeniable.

Very few human beings who gaze upon a crop circle do not have a visceral or powerful experience.

DIANNA:

If I was called to use art in some form to explore symbols that might be healing for me personally, how could I go about designing symbols that would be healing for my own highest, best good, that I could sketch or scribble or paint, or make out of objects in nature and put in my home? How could I work with healing symbols that are about my future, starting with the present?

THE Z'S:

Well, this is going to depend very much on the way you create. All creatives or creators create differently. For example, the more logical or organizational-minded creator may go and find lots of symbols in the world that they greatly enjoy, and either replicate them or print them out, and then create a brand-new symbol that they intuit, made up of all these known symbols.

In some way they are researching the work they are doing. They are bringing a certain level of research, curation, and organization into the new creation. They are taking old, established symbols, weaving them into the fabric of this new symbol, and creating something new for the world.

A completely different approach from a completely differently minded and wired creative might be to simply sit and intuitively draw for two hours without a specific goal or intention. But just to draw and draw and draw and let whatever falls onto the page come through them.

Then there are those who might do a little of both. The way to approach the creation is going to be quite specific to the individual, for there is not one way. However, what we will tell you is to ask yourself, in any creative endeavor: Do you reach a point with what you are creating when you stand back and feel that you achieved what you needed? If the answer is no, then you keep going until you do. And sure, take breaks, but if you are trying to bring through a healing frequency with your symbols, then knowing how to access that healing frequency in yourself will be first and foremost.

You may choose to play high-frequency music while you are creating. You may choose to curate the room where you are creating intuitively. You may want to draw on a great deal of light and existing symbols that mean something to you so that you can become a conduit and a vessel for new symbols.

Each creator is going to create differently. But the important thing to remember is that, as you are creating these symbols — or anything that is high frequency — getting yourself into a high-frequency state, as well as cultivating a high frequency in the environment in which you are creating, will of course always amplify the experience and the result.

DIANNA:

I appreciate you sharing how to work with symbols on a personal level. If we get more comfortable working with them in our own lives, it will help us with the channeling of new symbols needed in the world.

THE Z'S:

Symbols are harmonizers, as are certain pieces of music and certain sounds. Perhaps it is hearing birds or the purring of a cat that harmonizes you and resets something inside you.

The symbol that you see and take in through your eyes has the ability to harmonize your body. But so too can an abstract painting that brings you to a "sense memory."

Symbols are very important for the heart and all the chakras, but each different visual symbol will mean something different to each person. Of course, some will be more resonant than others.

DIANNA:

I agree. One more way I would like to talk to you about how we experience multidimensional communication is by discussing exit points. I will first define what an exit point is from my perspective.

An exit point is a moment in time when you can physically die and your soul can exit your body. I've had numerous experiences with exit points from an early age. Some people say we each have a certain number of exit points in our life. If we're not happy with the way our life is going or something changes, this is a moment we have set up in advance when we might exit our life, leave our physical body, die. Are you familiar with exit points?

THE Z'S:

Yes. We've been talking about exit points for a long time.

DIANNA:

I know you often say, "It's easy to die." Is that what you mean? That when we're done, we die?

THE Z'S:

Yes. Exit points, from our perspective, are points that are pre-programmed all through your life, when you and your soul will negotiate whether this is the time for you to exit your life. There are multiple, if you like, "death points" in your life.

Of course, for many, that can bring up the fear of death that is woven into your culture. Often, fear of death is really the fear of grief.

Your exit points are preprogrammed to give you "upshift" moments. It may sound somewhat strange that an exit point gives you an uplift, but they are often moments when you have a breakthrough or clear a hurdle in terms of your learnings on Earth. Even though they may sound like precarious windows in which you can leave your body, they are usually programmed at points in your life when you're going to have a breakthrough, reach a new level in your learning, or move on to a new phase.

So, let's say you are thirteen years old, and you get halfway through that year, and you are hovering near one of your exit points. It doesn't mean that there is a high chance you *will* die at that moment. It is just that as you approach the exit point, your soul gets to check in with you and your life and decide whether this would be a good time to exit the planet or not.

But exit points are never just personal. What is always taken into consideration is not just *your* life, but the lives of those who you will leave behind: Will your death have a positive, impactful effect on those closest to you or around you? Also,

an exit point will sometimes be taken not necessarily because *you* were complete with everything you needed to
learn on a human level, but instead because you had com-
pleted *enough* and it was deemed that if you were to exit
at this moment in time, a lot of the group around you and
people closely connected to you would benefit in some way.
Of course they would grieve and mourn, and loss would be a
big part of their experience at that time. But if it is the perfect
time for them to let you go, and in some ways, become more
of what you were embodying at that time — if it will serve
the group's growth or consciousness — then that will be
the point when you will choose to exit.

To clarify, we are not saying that you will suddenly be
"bumped out" of your body just because it's good for everyone around you; it can never work *that* way. But equally, your
death is not just about you. Most of you (though not every
single person on the planet) are connected to a number
of people for whom your death will be a significant awakening moment in their lives. The timing for all is always considered.

Now, you may say, "I don't remember the exit point when I
was thirteen." Most of you are not conscious of them. But
you become conscious of them when you have either a near-
death experience, an accident, or a time in your life when
you feel things are a little strange or a little close to the veil.
Some of you may have a sense that you are hovering around
an exit point — perhaps death is very much around you; perhaps you feel a little more "out of your body"; perhaps there
have been more trials and tribulations. It doesn't necessarily

mean you will take the exit point and jump through the death window, but you're aware that the possibility is moving in and around you at that time. That is what we refer to when we speak of exit points.

DIANNA:

I would like to share one of mine because it has a few questions in it that I think we could talk about and expand on. But before I share that story, I will say, it's very hard for us here in third-dimensional Earth to ever see death as a good thing. The thought of viewing losing anyone we have loved or love as a possible growth and learning opportunity is a pretty hard perspective for us to embrace here on Earth. Which is what creates (I think) a lot of the fear and the grief that you spoke of.

THE Z'S:

That is understandable because from a oneness perspective, if all were in spirit, there would be no loss. But because so many of you are experiencing spirit through the physical body, if a soul leaves the physical body, the soul will never again be the same.

Many of you have incredible communication with loved ones who have passed over, and that is beautiful, but after death, the loved one is not the same. They are not the same personality. They are not the same density. When a loved one passes on, those of you who can communicate with them beyond the veil (as it were) typically experience a lighter, brighter, wider version of their soul. So, death always means a loss of the human, and that is not to be avoided or to go ungrieved.

But what hurts when a loved one dies is the severing of your attachment to them, for you have (in some ways) merged with them, grown together like roots of a tree. You have merged your roots with the roots of this other human being. So, when they are taken off the Earth, what you feel is a disconnection from the harmony, from the balance, from the love, from the joy, from the nurturing, from the feeding that you were receiving from that relationship. So, a loved one's death is never an easy process for any of you to go through.

Even for those who have come to terms with the physical death of a loved one, there is still an energetic shift that moves through their body that, for even the fastest person, takes at least four to twelve weeks. For most, it can take several years, especially if they were in no way prepared for such a loss. But what happens afterward is what is interesting for all of you.

You might be grieving and mourning the loss of a loved one who, from your perspective, died too young. But what you are not aware of is that this death will leave room for someone else to come into your life. And we are not saying that is better or that replaces the person who died, but what we *are* saying is,

> *death always leads to a birth — either a birth*
> *of a new you, a birth of a new future,*
> *or a birth of a new scenario.*

The grief is real because you lose the form of the soul that you had become attached to and entwined with. But at the same time, for many of you, the presence of death in your life is a reconnection to the plane of spirit. This is why mediumship is so popular on your planet. Those who are skeptical of what you might call spirituality or the world of energy are able to overcome that skepticism through the death of a loved one from whom messages can be relayed.

This is not just about reconnecting with someone you love. This is about safely connecting with the world of spirit because of someone you love. For many people, the death of a true love or a dear loved one is a form of spiritual awakening, even if it is accompanied by a certain level of grief or loss or a shift in identity. But then you could argue that that is the same as any spiritual awakening that happens without the death of a loved one. You go through a certain grief, a shift of identity, a certain loss in order to have a different connection to this spiritual life that you are living. And *that* is something that death always facilitates.

Not everybody experiences this eye-opening side of death, but it is the highest opportunity for those who lose a loved one through death.

DIANNA:

Since the conversation we're having right now is focusing on communication, I want to address something you said in that last comment before I move on to my exit point experience.

I've always been able to hear messages from loved ones that I'm to convey to a person. To be honest, I'm often hesitant to do it, but they're always the simplest, most beautiful messages. They're very image oriented, object oriented — reminding them of a favorite flower or food, something simple that I wouldn't necessarily have known.

How am I hearing that? Who's giving me that information? Often, I'm not looking for it; I'm not asking for it. I may just be standing there having a conversation with someone and I hear, "Please tell them this." Very often, if I don't know this person, I really hesitate to relate the message because I think they're possibly going to be very concerned with what I'm doing and what I am saying. But clearly, I'm hearing something from somewhere. I've yet to not be accurate in the few times I've shared it. So, what is it? Where's it coming from?

THE Z'S:

Well, firstly, you are psychically receptive to others.

When you are having a conversation
with someone's aura, you are not just speaking
to that soul; you are speaking to all the
energies around that soul.

Look at what you are doing right now. With Lee's permission, you are speaking to us, who are around and in contact with his soul all the time, through him.

This is a conscious process. But what we will say is, you, like many intuitives or psychically gifted people, are able to hear those messages because the deceased souls realize you are someone whose ear they can reach. For example, you are speaking to your friend, and his grandmother (who is still around him) wants to get a message to him. She sees that you see her. You don't necessarily see her always in form, but you are aware of the width of his aura, and the width of his aura includes any loved ones, guides, or angels who are accompanying him.

It is no different from those who see people's guides and angels. The reason you are receptive to hearing that information is because you are taking in *all* of the person, not just what the person is presenting to you, which will be something many who are listening to or reading this experience.

The good news is, more and more these days,
people are more open to the world
of spirit because of the rise of consciousness
on the planet.

For most, the safest way to connect with spirit is through their deceased loved ones, the ones that they trusted before. Remember that the world of spirit has been painted as a foreign world to humans, which couldn't be further from the truth. Humans are walking through it every single day. If anyone is going to make a skeptical human feel safe about the existence of the world of spirit, it is one of the people they most loved and trusted who has now passed on.

So, *that* is why many of these relatives are getting your attention. It is not necessarily because *they* want to be heard; it is because they recognize you as someone who can facilitate a spiritual awakening for their loved one who they are hovering around and connected to.

DIANNA:

That's true because usually it offers enormous comfort to the person I say it to, and that is opening the door to this bigger conversation.

THE Z'S:

The beautiful thing about your question is, this is an area so many are hesitant about. But a good way to preface it is always to say, "I'm getting a message for you — that happens for me sometimes. It's a psychic message. Are you open to me sharing that with you?" At that point, you will find that *most* people will say yes, but it will at least tell them that you are about to go to a different frequency, so they can prepare themselves for that.

And the ones who are absolutely not open to that have the power to say, "No, thank you. I don't believe in that," or, "I don't want that message right now," in which case, you can respect their wishes. This is always a good way to, as you might say, test the waters to see how open to receiving the message the listener is.

DIANNA:

Thank you for that. I want to now tell you my exit point story. It happened about eight years ago. My husband and I were at a

wedding in another state. We really wanted to be at this wedding. It was a wonderful couple we know and love dearly. We
are very connected to them. On the morning of the wedding,
we had some free time. We took a drive, explored some of the
new town we were in, and had a great time. We were coming
back to the hotel to shower, change, pick up my mom, and
head off to the wedding.

My husband was driving, and we were on this very large, raised
highway — maybe three lanes on one side, merging with three
or four on the other side — and I heard the words, "Get over
now," very calmly, and I felt it gesturing. I felt the gesture
move my hand to the right. Without skipping a beat, I calmly
said to my husband, "Get over now," and I gestured to the
right.

My husband immediately moved our car just a few feet to the
right, and as soon as he did, a dark car sped by us, easily going
a hundred miles an hour. The driver shot directly across where
we had just been seconds ago and crossed numerous lanes
and exited down the ramp. If my husband hadn't immediately
moved the car to the right, if he had even so much as said,
"Why?" there is no doubt in our minds that that car would
have impacted us in such a manner that we would have spun
off that raised highway and most likely died.

My husband and I drove on quietly after that car sped by. And
as that visualization, "feeling" sense of what had almost happened sunk in, I started to shake deeply inside. All I could think
to say to my husband as we drove on was, "We almost died."
And he replied, "I know."

We got back to the hotel, dressed for the wedding, picked up my mother, and off we went. I did not stop shaking inside until I had been up and dancing joyfully with the wonderful small children at the wedding reception, and I was so grateful for that pure joy and spontaneity. But I kept thinking, "Whose voice did I hear?" and, "What dimension are they communicating with me from?"

THE Z'S:

That is your question?

DIANNA:

That's one of my questions. I could also ask: My husband and I are having this lovely experience — we're of high vibration, at a joyful place in our life. Why would I put an exit point here?

THE Z'S:

Ha! Well, firstly, the exit point in this case provided a teaching for you. Exit points are very useful. You see, in your case, you were ready to hear the psychic message, and a couple of different things were happening for you that day. It was not your time to go, which is why you were given the instruction, but it was also a deepening of your understanding that this was not your time.

The most significant thing here for you to understand is, you were given a message to steer you a different way at the right moment. Isn't it true that in recent years you have been listening more deeply to those messages that have steered you, even when they don't make full logical sense or, in the moment, you cannot see the full picture as to why you're receiving them? But also, your partnership with your husband, which was already strong in trust, gets stronger each time you both go through one of those moments.

This exit point was not as simple as "How nice that we didn't die because we were able to hear the intuition." It is a little more complex than that. How wonderful that you were able to hear. How good that your relationship encapsulates such trust that the smallest of gestures from you was met with unquestioning agreement from your husband, which enabled the two of you to quickly change course. Also, for you, it took being with the young ones in joy — moving and shaking everything through your body, letting the fear be released — to bring you back to the connection of life. For exit points always put you close to death.

When caring for someone who is approaching death or in long-term illness before death, you enter into the death realms. In much the same way, there is always a level of shock when you go through any brush with death. Because in those moments your body is preparing itself to exit, which is quite a dramatic experience energetically.

For you, it was not just *fear* of death that you were processing; it was the energetic impact of being that close to a death window. And it took time for you to settle again in your body. As we have said here, not only was it not your time to go, but it would also not have been the best time for your group either. This was significant for you in the long term of your life because it was one of several experiences that have been training you to listen to spirit at opportune moments. And *that* has been very helpful to you all through your life, and it's just a part of your lifetimes on Earth, as one who has always been able to hear and work with spirit in that way.

That is important both for your life and for the example that you set in many ways in your personal life and in your interactions — not just in this moment, in this conversation. And that is the truth for all of you. Any of you who are intuitive enough to hear that kind of message, to steer yourself onto the right track at the right time, it is not just about you and your learning. You become "in trust" with that energy in ways that you can then impart and share with others, and that is powerful.

That is how

> *consciousness and trust of intuition spread*
> *because more of you are beginning to work*
> *with it, be with it, know it, and recognize it.*

And the more that level of intuitive guidance and help gets recognized, the more the consciousness of humanity lifts above the old, programmed games that you as humans have been playing where you have been asked to *not* listen to the soul. Does that make sense?

DIANNA:

It does make sense. It's actually the core of what I'm trying to achieve with these conversations around communication:

How do we hear better to take back, regain, relearn the spiritual power of our multidimensionality?

THE Z'S:

The most important thing for all to remember is that, if you see us as an example of spirit (which would be a truth from your perspective), we are right here, right now. We are, in this moment, highly visible, highly audible. We are here with you. And this is how ordinary it can be, how easy it can be.

Of course, are there those who would be skeptical of this kind of conversation? Yes. And so they should be. This is not for them. This is not for their time in life or their way of connecting, so that is fine. But those of you who truly take in how, shall we say, "simple" this is, you are having not exactly an awakening but a remembrance of what is true. For we will say this again:

It is not that intuition or consciousness is just now coming to the Earth at these all-new levels; it is that those levels of intuition and consciousness are currently being unearthed on your planet. For they have been buried here for a very long time. There was a time in your more ancient history when they were more a part of your daily lives.

Rising now is an, if you like, information highway that you all have access to, that is coming to the forefront more. It does not mean that every single human being in their lifetime — in this lifetime — will become highly intuitive; that's not necessarily how it has to work. But it does mean that more and more people than ever before in the planet's history (certainly for the past five thousand years) are going to become aware of their connection to spirit in an all-new, undeniable way.

DIANNA:

I appreciate you saying all that, and it touches on a few last points with my story. I remember asking my husband afterward, when we got back to the hotel and we could take a minute and look at each other, "Why did you immediately move the car to the right? Why didn't you say, 'I'm sorry, what? Why?' — something along those lines, which would have been natural?" He said, "It felt like *your hand* moved the steering wheel."

He didn't feel it was him. Perhaps it was some force energy from me — maybe from my commitment, from the guidance I was getting, I don't know. But he said it didn't feel like it was so much *his* decision as he let it flow through him and some energy moved the car to the right. Which takes me to the part I want to get back to one last time: Whose voice did I hear? Was that my higher self? Was that a guardian angel? Is there a word, a description that explains who I heard?

THE Z'S:

This is *our* perspective of events, so it may be different from yours: You heard yourself. But you heard yourself relayed

from your guide team. As an example, we will break it down
this way: When Lee speaks to us, he has a very direct experience of us being an "other" voice — not the voice of his head,
not the voice of his higher self. He is very aware of when it is
us, the Z's, that he is speaking to. He has had this relationship
specifically with me, Zachary, for over twenty years at this
point, where he has been audibly hearing us as a separate
voice coming from above the left side of his head.

But occasionally he hears his higher self and his soul. That
is a voice that is not so distinct or different from his own.
So, what we see happened for you in that moment was, your
guide team knew that you needed to be redirected quickly
because the timeline that this other car was potentially
bringing your way was not your timeline. So, your guide
team relayed a loud message to move that you heard inside
your own head, in your own voice so it wasn't too alarming.
And that is how you experienced it.

Now, you may have perceived it somewhat differently, but
that is how we see the way it played out. The reason that
your husband felt no separation from the impetus you felt
is because by that point, you and he had already developed
a very good energetic connection that bypasses the mind.
The mind is involved sometimes, yes, but very in sync, with
very little resistance to each other. And so, he felt that im-
pulse through you because he tends to take physical cues
from you.

One of the dynamics of your particular relationship is that
you provide a certain physical impetus to his physical body.
There are other things he provides you, but that is one of the

aspects of your effect on him. In that moment, because your spiritual power was the loudest voice in the car, that's what he heard and that's what directed his body. Your spiritual voice is not a voice he is afraid of; it is a voice he knows very well.

Now, if you were in a relationship where this had never been practiced, never been developed, was completely new, he may have reacted in a slightly more, shall we say, questioning way, which, as you yourself said, would have resulted in a *very* different outcome.

DIANNA:

When I think of "outcome," I think of what you said about the group — this affecting the group. Because the hardest part of this (believe it or not) was not that I almost died or my husband almost died — because there was a part of me that thought, "Well, we would have gone together," and that, in some ways, was comforting. It's when I got to the wedding and...I get emotional just saying it now. I thought our not being there could have ruined this beautiful moment — not because we're so special; just that it would have been clear something was wrong because we are a very close group. And for my husband and I not to show up at that wedding, there would have been this very dark cloud emotionally, like, "What happened to them? Where are they?" Oh, that was the hardest part for me.

THE Z'S:

Yes. Not only would that have been a deeply impactful and negative event for the group at the wedding, but you and your husband were also designed to offer guidance to this married couple in later years. That is another reason that your exit point would not have served them. Not only would it have negatively impacted their wedding day, but it also would have removed you from your purposeful role in their future, which you are now playing out and will continue to. But look at how powerful that moment has become for you in a multidimensional way, and it is now a powerful moment to share with a group who will all be taking their own lessons from it.

This is what we mean by the spiritual power of exit points. There has been healing through this one for you. There has been learning through this one for you. There has been awareness through this one for you.

To circle back — yes, of course, the loss of a loved one on Earth is a painful experience for a human being, but from our perspective death is not a negative experience because it is not a negative experience for the person who dies. For those left behind who were not anticipating the death and are shocked by the removal of someone they loved, the death is not what you would call a positive experience in the moment, but it does offer layers upon layers of healing and learning. If we were to play out the scenario that you *had* died that day, would it have been understandably perceived as a tragedy for your family and for the day on which it happened? Absolutely, without question. Would it have sent them all in different directions of healing? Absolutely, without question.

Of course, there are those who can deny the healing and go down a destructive path. Some people who cannot deal with that level of pain or trauma may self-destruct in ways that are very harmful to themselves and others. But for many, it will set them on a path of having to open their heart, shed some grief, shed some tears.

While we are not saying that the death of a loved one is a desirable experience or one without impact, we are again just reminding you of the *power* of when those death windows hit your life, either through actuality — because you do pass over or someone you love passes over — or through what you sometimes call a "brush" with a death window. When someone you love almost dies and then they don't, you have a whole new level of heart appreciation and consciousness around their life and their presence. And equally for yourself, the same is true — a brush with death changes you forever.

DIANNA:

Well, it changed me, and I'm so grateful I'm working with communicating multidimensionally more and more. I hope our conversations around these topics inspire people to be more open. How would you say it? More embracing of what might seem like a scary way to communicate?

THE Z'S:

We will go back to what we have said a couple of times in this and the prior conversation: This information and communication is around you all the time. You just aren't necessarily seeing it. In much the same way, if you looked through a microscope at the room you are in right now, you would be shocked at all you would see through that microscopic lens that your naked eye was not picking up or perceiving.

Anyone who has been around Lee, or us through Lee, in the past two decades will have heard him laugh about how many times we have told people that it's very easy to die. It is very easy to die as a human being. And we know that for some of you, that is scary or morbid or triggering. But we say it so many times, and encourage Lee to talk about it at times when he is giving a spiritual talk or a teaching, because it reminds you to be in the present.

You see, so many forget that you never know what day you are going to die. When people suddenly receive a terminal diagnosis — told they don't have much longer to live, whether it is a few days or a few years — it changes them. It changes the way they focus their priorities. It changes the way they engage with life and with people. They suddenly become very…guess what? Present. And that is what we were talking about earlier: that you as a planet are moving into becoming more present, but that has to be a practice for many of you.

The gift of remembering that you can die
at any time is that you truly allow yourself
to be fully alive more of the time.

But if you've got it in your head that you're going to be alive for the next forty years and this next two, three years is about you perhaps building your work in the world or building your family, and then X, Y, and Z are going to happen — while those plans, visions, and dreams are all wonderful, hold them all lightly and remember to mostly live in the present. Because you never know what twists or turns life is going to take.

And so often, many of you are building the future from the past, either from past ideas that were given to you or past dreams of yours that you haven't updated. The one thing that happens for all of you as human beings is you keep changing and growing as you get older. So, your visions and dreams need to be updated accordingly as you go.

One of the most powerful ways to live is to remember that there *is* a physical end point to this human identity you are now in. You have never been this human identity in any of your previous soul lifetimes, even if you've incarnated many, many times. You are uniquely this person that you are right now, and when you physically exit from this body and this lifetime, you will never be this person again. So we say,

as much as you can, enjoy the experience
of being alive now. Tell people what you feel
you need to tell them. Show them what you
need to show them. Live in a way that
lights you up as much as possible.

We understand that there are restrictions in life — perhaps in your life right now or where you are living or the culture you are in — but within those restrictions, within the limitations of being human and belonging to a certain culture or a certain role that you are in right now, there is always a light in your heart or a peace in your heart that can be found. It is often in the simplest moments. It is often the simplicity of watching the butterfly move through the sky and recognizing the divinity in that.

"Live!" is always our message when we remind you that it is very easy to die and that you have these preprogrammed exit points. For many of you, especially those of you who live in fear of death, if you really stop and think about it, realizing that you might even have as many as a hundred exit points all through your life somewhat takes the fear away. Meaning, much of the time you're a little closer to death than you realize anyway. It's only going to be one day in your life that you truly take that exit point and make it real.

When that day comes, it will be the day that is most aligned for you and for the people you're leaving behind, despite the fact that it will cause grief for some. When you are no longer there, they will grieve over how much they loved you, and they will realize how influential and important you were in their life. The gap that you leave will truly, viscerally show people that. And that is the beauty of grief. It is actually an acknowledgment of the love and the space that someone filled up in another's life.

While we understand that grief is so often a painful and difficult process, it is also an acknowledgment of the power of a soul on Earth, an illumination of how that soul deeply affected others' lives, and a reflection of how its absence leaves loved ones altered. And that recognition moves a high level of spiritual awareness through the being who has lost the one they love. Even if it is painful awareness at first, it is the awareness of the power of the illuminated soul.

That is why, when you see a dead body, it doesn't make sense to most of you. You are looking at a lifeless body. You are no longer looking at the being that you used to know that inhabited that body because the soul, and the animation that the soul gives to a body, is everything.

That is why those who believe you are just a body, and that the soul is not its own entity, are missing an important piece of how that body becomes animated, and the color that comes through that body from the soul, and the uniqueness of that. So, when the soul leaves the body, you are left with very little of the person you remember — just a representative form that reminds you of who they were because the soul has now left the building.

DIANNA:

It feels very wonderful right now to think of the power of living in the present as an illuminated soul. Thank you for a great conversation.

THE Z'S:

Thank you. And all of you here will, as you read or listen to these conversations, perhaps feel an alignment or an upliftment. Some of you may heal a little. You may notice some movement in your mind or your emotions as a result of the conversations. That is OK; you are just clearing something from your field in response to something you heard or the way you interpreted what you heard. You will be serving your healing through that.

But many of you will notice an upliftment or an attunement to the frequency that we are emitting from. That is yours. While this conversation may have facilitated that, and hearing the dialogue between Dianna and us has created an opportunity for that, that frequency that you are feeling now is yours. As we have said many times, the consistent attunement to that frequency is what will normalize and stabilize it in your life. Also, you may need to work even more to maintain that attunement when you are around lower or more challenging frequencies for long periods of time.

We are only highlighting through this conversation what already exists. The work for humanity is to continue to galvanize that attunement in your daily lives so that it becomes more of your "normal" on Earth. And the more you do that for yourself, the more you naturally invite others into that frequency. That is how consciousness spreads and grows.

Good. A pleasure to be with you.

In peace and in love to all.

Chapter Five

CONVERSATION EIGHT

Topics

- How Lee, Dianna, and the Z's work together to create these conversations
- The nature of angelic beings
- The connection between the Z's and Sirius
- How the Z's communicate with Dianna
- Lee's process when channeling these conversations
- The Z's' reflections on the conversations so far

CONVERSATION EIGHT

DIANNA:

Welcome back to *Conversations with the Z's*. Today, we're going "behind the scenes" with the Z's. Welcome, Z's.

THE Z'S:

Good. Welcome.

DIANNA:

In today's conversation, I thought it would be fun to share more of the story of how we work together. I want to start by explaining one of the challenges for me when choosing questions to ask you all. That challenge is juggling my curiosity with what I feel the majority of the audience would benefit from hearing. For example, if I had followed just my curiosity in our first conversation, when you said you were one of eighty-eight beings and some of you had been incarnate on Earth before, I would've liked to ask you to tell me where each of the eighty-eight beings that make up the Z's are from, which of them had previously incarnated on Earth, and whether any of them were ever someone historically famous, perhaps living a life as Pythagoras or Alexander the Great or Mozart. I roughly calculated that might have been about ten hours of conversation, so I restrained myself! But I do still have a few questions I would like to ask: First, you said some of the Z's are from the "angelic realms." Could you explain what the angelic realms are?

THE Z'S:

Yes, but as you yourself just alluded to in reference to asking about the origin of each of the eighty-eight parts of us, the Z's, that could take many hours. So, we will do some broad strokes for you. The angelic realms — like many other realms and groups of beings or entities, on or off Earth — have within them many different factions. For example, some of you listening have angelic beings who are very much your guides. Meaning, you will be hearing from them, sometimes verbally. They will be more "parental" toward you than other angelics.

Lee's angelic team essentially channels and connects with other groups of angelics as required. Two of them are in our group of eighty-eight, but then they have contact with twelve other angelics if needed. Those two are positioned around him, and one of them relates very strongly to his body and his physical health, while the other relates to his emotional well-being.

His angelics are part of our group. They are part of the group named the Z's (incidentally, it was Lee's human listeners who came up with the term "the Z's" for this group). But there are other humans on the Earth or reading this who have what you might call more "instructive and communicative angelics," angelics who are somewhat parental and guiding figures. Because of the way Lee's guide team is organized, his angelics perform specific crucial roles, without which Lee would not be allowed or able to do what he is doing right now.

One of the angelics takes care of balancing Lee's physical health, and this can include drawing his attention to certain individuals, certain supplements, certain needs he has on Earth. His physical angel can help him find the right doctor or practitioner or the right type of supplement that could be good for him at the right time. If a friend is telling him a story that's important to his physical health, the angelic being will amplify his awareness. It will alert his body a little so that he suddenly pricks up his ears and pays attention to, say, a magnesium supplement story. Something about the magnesium supplement story gets his attention, or so he thinks. Actually, what his angelic has done is "surged" his attention, surged his energy field in a way that heightens his awareness so that he's receiving an angelic message about increasing the magnesium in his body, for that is what is needed right now.

Emotional well-being is the role of Lee's other angelic. This angel is aware of Lee's need for emotional well-being, which is also very important for many of you reading this. Emotional well-being is high on your priority list. This is not to say that it shouldn't be for all humans, but there are some of you whose sensitivity relies on emotional balance, and Lee is one of those. So, his emotional well-being angel will not only work to rebalance his energy directly but will also nudge his attention and his awareness and surge his energy field so that he has an "epiphany moment" whenever he needs to follow a certain thread or call a certain friend or reach out for help in a certain way or perform an activity that will calm him down. You see, as humans, you often interpret these moments of epiphany or awareness as coming from your mind, your heart, or your instinct, but actually you are usually being nudged by an angel.

Lee is a little unusual in having eighty-eight beings on his guide team, for the majority on Earth do not have such a broad team. But then they do not need such a broad team, for Lee's team is also "broadcasting." Part of Lee's role on Earth is to be a bridge for others, for their own spiritual connection and connection with other realms. So, the organization of his guide team is quite specific. But to choose one of your listeners or readers as an example: You may have nine to twelve guides around you, and perhaps three of them are angelics. And two of those angelics perform similar roles to the ones we just described Lee's angelics as having. But perhaps your third angelic is a little more like Zachary — meaning me, the spokesperson for the Z's. This angel is more of a guiding force, more of a presence that "whispers in your ear" messages and words. You see, there are different levels and roles within the angelic realm, and each human on Earth will have access to the angelic realm that suits their individual path.

As we pointed out, Lee has clear access to a team of guides (us) that is very strong for him. So, he does not need a guiding angel or an angel from what you might call "the higher ranks." However, we don't like this phrase, for again, on Earth there is the perception that if you are a higher rank, you are superior to someone who is of what you would call a lower rank. And that is actually not at all how it works. You are all needed. Every single person playing their role allows every other person to play their role. So, this egoic-superiority

idea, which is woven into the minds of humans and has limited your potential for a very long time, is a tricky one. But
our point here is that there are different levels of angel. And
there are the angels whose role it is to be a little more of a
mentoring, guiding, and sometimes verbal presence in your
life. And then there are other angelics who work purely in an
energetic way.

It is similar to the group of friends you have. There are some
friends in your life that you feel physically safe with, because
they are hyperaware about the safety of bodies. Their own
angelic imprint shows through in their personality. And
then there are other friends who you go to for mentoring
or advice, but they're not necessarily the ones you would go
on holiday with to laugh. So, similarly, the members of the
angelic realms are all very different and multilayered.

*All of you, without fail, have angelic beings
around you, assigned to you, working with you.*

Some of you have more than others, but most people on
Earth do not have more than four angelics around them,
with the exception of those people on Earth whose job it is
to commune with large groups of angelic beings. And many
of these are in public positions where they speak about their
connection to angels. It is not that they are special, but the
reason that they have a magnitude of angelic consciousness
and angelic connection is so that they can impart that to
everyone else. And their imparting of that, in some ways,
seeds more angelic connection on the planet, just as this role
that Lee has right now is helping seed others with their own

connection to spirit. They don't need to be connected to us, the Z's. We are helping to seed their connection to their own guides, their own spirit on Earth. Did that answer your question?

DIANNA:

Yes, but I want to go a little further with it. The angelic hierarchy that you're talking about (and I understand that "hierarchy" is not the word that's ideal for this), does that include what are known on Earth as the Seraphim, the Cherubim, the Thrones, Archangels, and so forth?

THE Z'S:

Yes. However, what you are describing is a useful understanding for people, and it is not an untrue understanding, but it tends to cut out a great deal of angelic energy. A couple of things we should say here: First, much of your angelic understanding has been handed down across the centuries. And while much of it remains true, angelic presence on Earth has (in fact) grown, especially in this past hundred years. The angelic presence on Earth has become stronger. So, often when you hear about light or consciousness rising on the planet, what people are actually becoming aware of is an enormous number of angelic beings who are now able to, we will say, incarnate closer to Earth than ever before. So, the hierarchy you are describing as laid out in many different descriptions, books, and teachings is true. But what we would like to draw your attention to is that the angel is not so separate from the human. In other words,

in the past hundred years, a "merge"
has been happening between humans
and angels on Earth.

This may seem outlandish to some of you, for you would argue that right now, in your human history, you are in a very tumultuous time, where the dark seems to want to rear its head. But that is also why the angelic energy is getting stronger on Earth. In the past hundred years, a new realm of angelic being has started to form on Earth as a result of this human-to-angel connection. And we will say that crystalline energy is the conduit for this fusion of human and angel. There are many humans walking around today who, you will notice, have a very strong angelic presence. Many of them have to overcome their dislike of this planet, their dislike of the darkness, their issues with the violence, and the lack of harmony. For the angelic nature not only supports and nurtures harmony; it *is* harmony.

If angelic beings lose their sense of harmony, they die. They die off from the form that they are in, which is not (as you know) a physical form. But much as the soul of a human can go through many incarnations, so too can angelic souls shift and change over time. So, what you are seeing right now on Earth in this past hundred years (and especially since the turn of the twenty-first century) is more and more angelic and human "twinning" taking place. At the moment, it is why so many of your sensitive people (souls) — and especially young sensitive souls — are leaving the planet. Many of them are choosing to end their lives or are finding their lives suddenly ending in dramatic or difficult ways, and it causes a ripple of distress among your people as you witness it happening. Many of these sensitive souls are literally too sensitive for this Earth, but they are the beginning of a new phase that we would call "the era of the human angel" that is coming into being.

Many of you might hear that phrase and separate from it and think, "Ah, how lovely is that? How nice that more angels are coming to Earth." You forget that all of you have angelic energy in you and available to you. These human angels we are speaking of are more of a fusion; the crystalline energy on the Earth is beginning to allow a fusion between human and angel — a closer relationship. And these are often the leaders of consciousness where kindness, noncruelty, and the support and understanding of sensitivity are concerned. They are often artistic in nature, and most of them are highly introverted.

This doesn't mean there aren't some extroverts out there, but extroversion in the extreme tends to be when someone is incapable of living in their inner world. However, extroversion is a very important role. Some of your greatest extroverts have played very important roles on the planet. So, we are not in any way saying extroverts are "less than" by being that way.

But of the highly introverted new angelic humans being born, very few of them are older than twenty-four or twenty-five at this time. The vulnerable period for these souls is the second half of their teenage years. That is the period when they are truly coming to terms with what this world is and how it has been constructed, and they find themselves alien-ated by it. Many of them don't make it through that stage. For this Earth (at this moment in time) still does not have enough angelic consciousness seeded into its structure. As we have said, many of these teenagers have ended their lives, for they cannot quite handle the energetics of their role. We understand the tragedy for those of you who lose those lives, and we honor that. The grief must be felt.

But it was always known that this new human-angel par-adigm was going to be a tricky, uphill swim for many. So, more souls than were required were elected to come and play that role. It is like the "mating game" between humans: only one sperm will fertilize the egg, and the others will not make it. It is a similar energetic uphill swim for these an-gelic human souls, but more and more of them are break-ing through now. And by the time you get to the end of this decade in which we are having this conversation — so, by 2030 — you will find there will be less difficulty with this angelic human dance.

We did not in any way mean to dismiss your question, Dianna, and we do appreciate what you are bringing to the audience's attention. If you are interested in the hierarchy of angels as it has been noted for some time, by all means, research what is already there. But our main message and what you gave us permission to speak about through your question today is to draw your attention to this, if you like, new breed of human angel that is coming through. The rea-son we gave you the title *The Energetics of the New Human Soul* [the title of Book One of *Conversations with the Z's*] is because that is exactly what we are speaking about in all these conversations so far. We are speaking about the new version of humanity on the planet in this century. And one aspect of that is these human angelics who are fused via crystalline energy more so than ever before.

You will have more human angels on the planet than ever before in Earth's history, and they are very important to ushering in the sensitivity of this time. It does not mean they will all be the architects of everything in this time, but they will be a very important piece. As you move from one paradigm that is far more hierarchical into a paradigm that is more based in oneness, they will be ambassadors for heart energy, sensitivity, and more importantly, the equality of all living beings.

Many of you are aware of who these young human angels are in your life. Reading our words, some of you immediately had visions of these young people that you know. Support them as much as you can. Be there for them, particularly while they're between the ages of fourteen and twenty. During those vulnerable years, many of these young, open souls are trying to deal with a world where they do not see a place for their openness to reside.

DIANNA:

You immediately made me think of a book I enjoyed reading very much by Dolores Cannon called *The Three Waves of Volunteers and the New Earth*. She crossed over in 2014, but she has an amazing body of work as a hypnotherapist and had thousands of cases that she studied of people sharing past lives and so many other interesting aspects. I highly recommend the book, because it sounds like you're describing these young people. She would've said that they are the "third wave," that they are here to do just what you said, and that they are very fragile in some ways and crystalline. So, it was a very interesting comparison, hearing you say that. Now, that said, I do want to —

THE Z'S:

May we interject?

DIANNA:

Yes, please.

THE Z'S:

We really appreciate this sidebar because it gives us an opportunity to speak about Dolores Cannon for a second. This is a good thing for those of you who are trying to understand your role and tend to grapple with it. Energetically, Dolores Cannon carried what many of you would understand as emperor energy. She held the role of an emperor in prior lifetimes. She commanded armies and people and had a very tough time and was quite a tough character in some of her earlier lives.

It's important for you to understand that those tough lifetimes are what made it possible for Dolores to help seed light, love, and understanding on the planet in this lifetime. She had to have lifetimes where she was, shall we say, elevated above other people in order to allow her to be an ambassador of such radically opposing information, at a time when the information she was bringing was not necessarily welcomed by all. And in the worst cases, it was mocked or rejected by all.

We want you to understand that it was Dolores's ability to be "tough" that allowed her to bring that love and light through. If she had not had a foundation in other human lifetimes of being tough, being at the top of her tree, she would never have been able to deal with the psychic attack and the energetic and emotional attack she was often on the receiving end of, whether she was aware of it or not. What she stood for was very challenging and polarizing for some people, even though she was a great way-shower of your time. You don't necessarily have to agree with everything she said, but throughout her life — and the body of her work speaks for itself — she was here to open this planet. That was what she stood for, and she did it quite brilliantly.

Was she dealing with her own human personality healings? Yes. She had her own human lessons around sadness, around isolation, around feeling alone on the planet many times, which is not uncommon for those who play the emperor role. And most of you have experienced or will experience the emperor role in some parts of this life, in other lifetimes, or in your future lifetimes to come. And we bring that up to help you all understand your roles.

We know that throughout time, public figures, famous figures, people who you are all supposed to know the name of have drawn a lot of attention and focus. And up until now,

that has been useful and understandable within the hierarchical society you are in. But going forward, *everybody* can
be viewed as famous. And in fact,

you are the most famous person in your life.
Do you know why? Because you are the only
person who will know your life story
from beginning to end.

It doesn't mean other people won't experience you, have an
idea of you, but you should see yourself as the most important person in your life. For you are the most important person in your life in terms of your soul learning experience. We
don't mean you should belittle others or ridiculously inflate
yourself — that's a whole other personality "ism." No, we are
simply asking you to look at this woman, Dolores, see why
she did what she did, understand what she was dealing with
on a human level, and then see yourself in the same light.

There are things that you are doing in your
life, are compelled to do in your life, that
are about far more than just this life. They
are built on not only the seeds of your prior
lifetimes, but also seeds of cultural history.

So, Dianna, we appreciate you bringing focus to these young,
open souls and their deep sensitivity that, as you have quite
accurately pointed out, is explored within Dolores's messag-
ing and teaching.

And those of you who get stuck in the tragedy of the lost lives of those angelic souls who have taken their own life, or those of you who loved or knew someone who took their life because they were in so much pain, grieve, by all means. We encourage you to do that. It's important. It's part of the process. But understand the greater dynamics at play here, and perhaps use your grief to spur you on to ask yourself, "Who else might I know who reminds me of that person? And what could I do to perhaps ease their path, offer some help?" It might be that there is nothing you can do, but using your grief to change your future behaviors, change your future actions, is very powerful.

That is what grief can teach. It can teach you a new way to experience the present and the future, and a new way to act in the future as a result of your awareness of what you have lost.

When you lose something, you have an opportunity to both acknowledge what it meant to you and to consider whether you are going to approach your life in a different way going forward.

DIANNA:

Thank you for that. I have very much enjoyed the work of Dolores Cannon and encourage other people to look into it as well. I just want to go back to one thing before we move on from the angelic realms. You said that an angel could die off if they lose their sense of harmony. What do you mean by "die off"? Energetically, they return to their own form of soul, much like we humans do when we die?

THE Z'S:

Think of the caterpillar and the butterfly, two (from your perspective) wildly different beings, and yet you know they are deeply connected. Like caterpillars that transform into butterflies, there are certain souls that will graduate into the angelic realm if it is decided that they are able to access that level of frequency.

That is not for everybody, by the way. It is not necessarily the goal to enter into the angelic realm. Again, that is hierarchical thinking on Earth, for the hierarchy that religion has given you around angels has not necessarily helped everyone to understand the equality of all beings when it comes to the soul realms. You can, as a soul, graduate into the angelic realms for a brief period, which may be a thousand years in Earth terms, or you may stay there for hundreds of thousands of years, if that suits your role and what you are doing.

But equally, there are those who come to the end of their time in the angelic realm, and they graduate to something else. We used the word "die," but we don't necessarily mean a death in terms of an ending; it's more a transformation. We will give you an example: There are several angelics right now who are resigning from their old role as more and more of these human angelics are being born on Earth. There will be less need for nonhuman angels. We're not saying they won't be there — they will. But as more and more are born on

Earth, there is also a need for the "old guard" to change and transform, for everything is in motion and transformation in the Universe, always. So, some will graduate from being in the angelic realm, and they will, in many cases, move out of Earth's orbit and move into different parts of the Universe where their roles are somewhat different — where the angelic energy is not so needed. You see,

angelic energy is very specific to Earth.
It is the realm in which humans can connect
with love, healing, and oneness.

From an Earth perspective, you can see angelic energy as the window through which you can enter healing, support, love, oneness. The angelic being becomes the window through which a human can connect to each of these frequencies.

The idea that angelic beings can graduate after a period of time is one of the, shall we say, somewhat tricky things for humans to get their heads around. It may help to think of it this way: Many people will take great comfort in the idea that the human person Dianna and the human person Lee are sitting here having a conversation, and there are eighty-eight fixed beings that they are having a conversation with that I am the one spokesperson for. But of course, none of that's really true. For Dianna herself is a thousand things, and Lee himself is a thousand things. And even though we, the Z's, are formed as a cluster of eighty-eight beings, we have access to thousands upon thousands of other beings.

The infinite nature of everything can be a little difficult for the human mind to grasp. And that is why pieces of information are given on Earth, as required. It would not make any sense for most human beings to suddenly see the map of the Universe and how it is orchestrated today. And that is not because they are not intelligent enough to grasp it; it's because it would completely eradicate their understanding of the form they are in right now. That would not be useful at this point in time. However, pieces of that information, pieces of that map are *highly* appropriate and allow you to expand, without annihilating or obliterating you.

To recap, with angelic beings, there are many who graduate after many thousands or even hundreds of thousands of years, when it is decided that the next step in *their* soul's evolution is to transform into a being that has a different role, a different form.

DIANNA:

Thank you. That's fascinating. It gives us a lot to think about, especially since we've all grown up with certain perceptions. Now my curiosity is going to take me in another direction, and I hope you'll bear with me because this is for you, Zachary. You said you were connected to Sirius. I am wondering if that is a star, a planet, or a greater constellation, and what does it mean to be from or connected to Sirius?

THE Z'S:

Very good question. We will say (for this is our truth) that from our perspective, Sirius is a constellation, but most on Earth would understand it as a star, and that is not incorrect.

But one focal point of one star is far more than one star, if you understand what we were just saying a moment ago.

Now, a couple of things to elaborate on here: Sirius and Earth have been long connected where light, higher dimensions, and particularly the third eye and telepathy are concerned. A great deal of Sirius energy was seeded in ancient Egypt. And from that place, it has spread across the globe in many different ways, partly because of certain historians, energy workers, and artifacts that have Sirius energy within and were taken to different parts of the planet. But there was a time when Sirius and ancient Egypt were in strong contact, strong connection — that is, before galactic war broke the connection between Sirius and Earth. And that is its own set of stories to do with your galactic ancient history, which is quite complex.

But the simple way for us to describe it is, Sirius is very much a part of this Earth and has been for a very long time. Sirian energy is seeded on this planet — has been for a long time — but is now somewhat buried underground. So, when you look at the crystalline energy and the crystalline grid within the Earth, Sirian codes are running through it, and they greatly support the development of telepathy and third eye vision, which means seeing the future, being able to co-create with the future, and being able to build higher energy lines and timelines for the future. The reason that *we* have such a strong connection to Sirius — and specifically myself — is that whenever we are transmitting to you like this or speaking to Lee, there is a line that runs from us to Sirius, then down to Lee on the Earth.

So, you are encountering Sirius energy whenever you are reading or listening to this communication. It is not 100 percent Sirius energy; it's a blend. However, if you want a number or a percentage, we could say that anything from 10 to 30 percent of the energy conveyed in these transmissions, in these conversations, is energy from Sirius. And that is why so many of you feel your third eye opening when you read or listen to these. Or afterward, the knock-on or ripple effect is you become more intuitive because you are tapping into a star that has the imprint of telepathy, the higher mind, third eye vision, and not surprisingly, communication. Sirius is very strong in communication on your planet. It is very strong in harmonic sounds. Your birds and your creatures — when they make noise, when they create their sounds — are often in resonance with and in relay to other planets, other stars. And Sirius is one of those.

There is a harmonic relay of sound between Sirius and Earth that shows up in a great deal of your music and in a great deal of the sounds created by nature. It is always interesting to us that so many of you think of alien life as "other" at all, for if you truly understand your position in the Universe, you are not separate from anything. It is just that you have not been shown these other planets or life-forms in any overt way. And in fact, certain parts of your world have worked hard to conceal them from people.

We are speaking to you at a time when much of that concealment is beginning to fall apart, and most of you in your lifetime will be very aware of your galactic connections as you go through life. But Sirius is particularly noteworthy because it's a big part of the specific frequency that comes through us and comes through Lee, and more importantly, that you are choosing to connect with through this conversation. I no longer live on Sirius, but I am of Sirius, from Sirius, and formed and forged in that energy field.

DIANNA:

I have also read that the Sirians are guardians for Earth. Is that correct?

THE Z'S:

One of them. There are eight different groups who are guardians for Earth, and we Sirians are one of them.

DIANNA:

Should we save the conversation about the other seven for our galactic conversation we'll have down the road?

THE Z'S:

It would be best, simply because talking about it now — not only the naming of the other groups but also the reasons behind the guardianship — would open a can of worms for you. But we should say this: We are guardians of Earth, and so are you, the reader or listener. Our ability to be guardians of Earth is no greater or less than any human individual's ability to be a guardian of Earth, once that human has woken up to the nature of their own place in the Universe as well as Earth and humanity's place in the Universe.

DIANNA:

I appreciate you reminding us of that because we do have a tendency to give our power away to what we perceive as higher beings. And you're absolutely right: all of us on this Earth at this time are guardians of this Earth.

THE Z'S:

Earth is a home for us too. Even though many of us *have* been embodied and incarnate as humans, because we are not embodied at this time it is very easy for you to see us as "other" or to see those from Sirius as "other." And yet there is but one home in the Universe. It doesn't mean all the neighbors get along. It doesn't mean there aren't fights between groups or planets, just as you see on Earth — there are. But the harmonic frequency of the Universe is far stronger once you are off Earth than many of you have been led to believe.

We are not saying that planetary war does not exist — it does. Galactic war exists. It is a real thing. However, many of you believe it is far scarier or darker than it actually is. And that is because you are *being led* to believe that so that you will continue to believe and support the dark stories that justify war on your planet. Simply because of the way the human mind has been programmed, any of us being called the "guardians of Earth" tends to make you think we are protecting you against some villainous force. And yet

there is nothing off Earth to be
more afraid of than some of the
most difficult energies on Earth.

And your Earth has been more galactic for a very long time than many of you have been allowed to understand.

DIANNA:

Thank you for that. I appreciate you going a little further on that subject, and I know we are saving that for a time when we can go even deeper and take our time and pace it better. Now, for a behind-the-scenes aspect of our current conversation, I do want to address some questions people ask me about my work with you. And one of those is, "How do I communicate with you? What does it feel like? Is it the same as it is for Lee?" No. My experience is, I feel like you're sitting across a table from me — we're just friends sitting across a table, having a discussion. That's the energy I feel. I don't feel you in my head, I don't feel you clustering around me, but I do feel like I'm talking to you across the table.

One time when I do feel that dynamic shift a little is late at night. I don't know if this is you — I've never asked you to answer this, Zachary — but at night, I tend to get up from 3 a.m. to 5 a.m. or 6 a.m. and do a lot of work. I've given up trying to get away from that pattern and have just embraced it. And as you have said, many other people do this too: we rearrange our lives to fit what works. But at night, sometimes, when I'm working, especially on conversation ideas, and thinking, "Where could we go next? What would be a creative way to explain that?" I'll run ideas through my head. And every now and then, just for fun, I'll say, "Z's, do you like that direction?" I feel I hear you say yes or no, and that you give me a little feedback. Is that you, or is that my higher self? Could you share your perspective on working with me?

THE Z'S:

Well, we reach you through your higher self. You have your own guide team, many of whom are highly psychic because that is part of the role you decided to play in this lifetime. You said you would come back and allow yourself to re-enter the psychic realms, even though much of your life looks a little more traditional or "normal human" to the outside eye. But you agreed to come in and be a wisdom keeper for the psychic realms, which is why you have always been so interested in researching them, not necessarily to learn, but to observe. You like to see what's out there and read between the lines of anything that you take in because you are evaluating, "What is the current cultural belief about this? What is the current mainstream information that's out there?"

We reach you through your own guide team. You have one that we will call the "oracle." We will not name this guide, for that is your private business, but we will say your oracle guide — your all-seeing eye — is the one who can communicate with any being and is the one through whom you go when you have interaction with any being outside yourself, including some of those apparition soul aspects, ghost children, or other beings that you come across. We can reach you better at night, for your soul is more open, and it is not just because you are in the nighttime hours; it is because the world around you is asleep and so you can put aside many of your roles.

Many of you who are reading or listening to this have anything from eight to sixteen roles that you are playing on a daily basis. These roles could include *mother, friend, daughter, counselor, employee* — there are so many different roles that make up who you are. And while there is a throughline for each of you in all your roles, each role requires something different of you: it requires a different way of interacting, and it may involve different people in other parts of your life. So, at nighttime, you can let go of many of those roles, even though at nighttime, you, Dianna, like many others, are sifting through events in some of those roles to find resolution. Perhaps something happened at work that day that you are a little bothered by, so at nighttime, you can get a clearer handle on moving some of the energy around it.

But yes, we can access you more at night because you are less encumbered by your human roles. When the world around you sleeps and nobody needs your energy or your presence or your time — and this is true for so many of you — you can have a more direct communication with the soul realms. So, you are right that whenever you are working on this project specifically, you are able to access us because we will be not too far away in case you need us.

And your oracle, if you like, is the telephone operator that connects your call to us and monitors it. Your oracle guide is fierce about what it will and won't let in. It has taught you a great deal about boundaries. You now teach boundaries to others a lot, but in your younger years, yours were a little less defined, for your openness and innate curiosity made you want to run into the world and explore everything. This is true of many open, gifted children. And it took you falling over several times to start to finally listen to your oracle and pay attention when your oracle was suggesting, "No, don't go there, don't go there. Go here instead."

DIANNA:

That is quite true. I have two more questions for you from a listener. The first one is, "Does Dianna know the Z's, or has she worked with any of them before, in other lifetimes?"

THE Z'S:

Yes and no. The yes part is because Dianna has been connected to several of our group in prior lifetimes but also in this lifetime. You see, even though we are a group, and we are dominantly assigned to Lee, if you think about it, we are also assigned to the hundreds of thousands of people on the planet who have heard us or used our messages and our frequency for their own evolution. And then of course, there is the unspoken energy that we are able to permeate through the planet. But Dianna and Lee have had many incarnations together. And so, there are aspects of Dianna's psychic self and energetic guide team that Lee recognized once he met her, just as she recognized parts of his guide team, even though the recognition was not overt between the two of them.

In the early stages of reconnecting in this life, of course, they were taking each other in on a human personality level. But actually, what was going on for both of them was a "twinning" in many of the areas where they overlap. Like all human beings, they have differences. They have areas where they don't necessarily connect, but there are a great deal of crossover connections between Dianna and Lee in terms of personality, energetic makeup, and also their roles at this time in their journeys on Earth. So yes, Dianna has had different interactions with different members of this group, but it is a little less past-history and a little more present-now.

DIANNA:

Thank you. And the second question I have from the listener is, "Did Dianna have an agreement before this lifetime to meet up with the Z's and Lee to record these conversations?"

THE Z'S:

Yes, she did, and that is actually how and why she hunted Lee down, which was uncharacteristic of her. But she did not know that their connection and their friendship would lead to these books. That required a gentle push from Lee, shall we say. But Dianna knew all of it at a soul level. She knew what was on the table and what was possible. But anyone can reject what is possible. Dianna could have said no, and Lee could have said no. This is how it works.

You have multiple opportunities to connect and cocreate and collaborate with people in relationship, in work. And if things align and everyone says yes, it happens. That is why these choices you make are so powerful: they literally alter the course of your future, but also your history. You see, the choices you make today can very much heal and reorganize and rebalance events that have happened in your life before now. So, the choice you make today can directly heal your past, even if you don't realize it.

Before this lifetime, Dianna and Lee made an agreement to have these conversations, and they have supported each other in different ways in their relationship and in their work together to be ready to do this together at this time. It may not seem like an enormous undertaking to sit and have conversations, but the actual recording of these conversations is the smallest part of this work. To then put these transmissions out into the world has a relay effect on both of them, on everyone who is involved. These books and conversations are worlds within a world. And so, you are creating a world of energy here that has its own life and will have its own life in all who come to spend a little time in this world to enhance their own world and their own way of working in the world.

So yes, there was an alignment, a soul contract, but it was unknown to both of them on a conscious level for at least the first few years. However, we are pleased to report that, during an intuitive reading that he gave Dianna very early on, Lee did in some ways preface this future, even though at the time he didn't understand he would be involved in these books or some of the books that Dianna would be creating.

DIANNA:

On a final note, I want to talk about what happens to me while I'm doing these recordings with respect to Lee. I am very protective of Lee in our recordings. He seems to go to a much deeper place in these conversations than if he's just doing an MP3, where he's alone and you're speaking through him. And he is also lighter in our private conversations when he is channeling you. These conversations take a lot more energy from him. I always keep one eye on the clock. Lee will give me a time when he wants me to check in with you to see how he's doing. He drinks an enormous amount of water — we stop for water breaks. I'd like you to share a little bit of this process with the listeners, just so they understand what Lee goes through.

THE Z'S:

Firstly, what you must understand — and this is an important piece — is that these conversations are very different from private conversations. They are not private conversations. They are public conversations that are being recorded in advance of the listeners and readers partaking in them. But as someone who is very in tune with the future (that is part of Lee's wiring), Lee can feel the impact of these conversations, even if he doesn't fully understand that in a conscious way while his body is transmitting them. It is a somewhat "blind" process for him. For even though he is not in what you would call a traditional trance, he is (right now) sitting behind, half listening to what is going on, but he does not have his listening capacity, for we are having to take over much of his mental faculty in order to do this. So, channeling these conversations has a big impact on Lee.

The other factor that we will mention is quite practical. Lee never channels for three hours when he records MP3s. Ha! He only ever needs to do about an hour or sometimes, in the longest ones, an hour and twenty minutes. And that is different from these conversations with you, for those shorter transmissions come more from the etheric plane. In these longer ones, he is bridging the etheric and human planes because you are asking human-minded questions that are designed to remain etheric and multidimensional but also to be grounded. Your intent (which is the correct intent for this collaboration) is to ground much of what we say. Therefore it is a different kind of stream.

So, these conversations are different. They require a bit more bouncing up and down, whereas, if Lee is simply channeling an hourlong transmission message from us, it is coming from a different dimension. That is why many people have an uplifting experience from those. But *this* is different, for it is both uplifting and grounded.

Sometimes one is better than the other. And for some listeners, they will prefer the more grounded or the more etheric. We personally believe a balance of the two is best, for it gives you all the opportunity to go up and down the rungs of the ladder.

Part of the reason it takes more energy for Lee to do this is simply because it takes more time. But secondly, it's because he is having to bounce up and down between the realms. And rather than simply flowing through his own body (which he can do when he is doing a transmission message from us), he is having to flow through his body *and* play a game of tennis with you as you serve different questions to us that bring our focus to different places.

So, yes, these conversations are more impactful on him because of the time and because of the dance between dimensions that these conversations allow, but it is also because these will be, shall we say, more heard, more consumed. More people will tune in for these, so therefore there is a stronger energetic impact on Lee as well as on the future of your lives. Each of you is also being the conduit for this, which may seem a little abstract today for each of you as you are doing it. But that is the truth of the future of these conversations, and therefore it is the future energy that you feel when you are in them.

The other piece we will throw in here is, it is also just another phase of Lee's evolution. Everyone goes through phases with their art, with their craft, with their mastery. And he is now going through a new phase with us that is happening at the right time and is built on the foundation of everything that came before.

DIANNA:

I appreciate you clarifying what he goes through. And it just makes me appreciate him all the more. I'd like to end, Zachary, with you telling me how you and the Z's feel the conversations are going. Are we achieving what you had wanted to achieve?

THE Z'S:

Ha! Well, you won't like our answer. Yes, we are pleased (to use your word), and we are achieving what we hoped we would achieve. And we will tell you right now, as we are ending conversation eight, we are 1 percent through this process! [Dianna laughs.]

We knew you would not like that, Dianna. For Dianna, this is just like the joke between you and Lee (and we hope you won't mind us disclosing this) where he is always teasing you that there are tens and tens and tens more books to come, and you are always telling him you don't want to do that many! And that is the way that you two tease each other about doing these. But in truth, we have now covered about 1 percent of the ground.

So, Dianna, we understand you are a diligent worker and a hard worker, and as you yourself will say, a recovering perfectionist. We don't want you to feel deflated by that — it is quite an achievement that 1 percent has been covered!

But we will say, we are enjoying these conversations. We are noticing that both you and Lee are calibrating to them more and more each time. Even though your conscious minds were calibrated from the word "go," there is an energy shift that is taking place, not just in you two, but also in the audience. Because you are both antennae for the audience as these conversations are taking place, you are also having to calibrate to the audience and their needs, intuitively.

If the two of you are willing to still be doing these conversations when you get into conversations twenty and thirty, you will be struck by where they go. For each of these conversations is a chapter in a potentially very large book, and how long these conversations continue will be up to you two and also the desires of the audience.

And by the way, if they stopped tomorrow, that wouldn't be a bad thing either. We don't want to set up any achievement goal for any of you here. But we will say that 1 percent has been covered, and we are expecting to get to *at least* 8 percent with you both before you decide whether to carry on and carry the mantle further, or whether it will be someone else's job on the planet to impart the same energy that we can as a group with you. Time will tell, and so will your soul contracts.

DIANNA:

Time *will* tell. [Dianna laughs.] I don't know what else to say to all that.

THE Z'S:

We would say: you can now go and have a nice rest — lie down and breathe. Ha!

DIANNA:

I need a nap. You're right. And I guess I'll be around when I'm about 110, working on the next conversation. I keep telling Lee that I don't think he has it pictured quite right, but —

THE Z'S:

That is why Lee keeps telling you, to both tease you and spur you along, that you are going to live into your hundreds. You have just entered your next decade and are now in the early part of your sixties. We hope you do not mind us disclosing your age, but the reason we do that is because it is important to share that on a personal level, your work is just beginning. You know this, Dianna. You have a whole lifetime of work behind you. There is so much that you have personally gone through and healed through, and you have also given a lot in many different areas all through your life. Yet here you are at the beginning of a couple of decades that are going to be profound and very important, not just for you, but for the people who will experience your work.

And by "your work," we mean, yes, work like this that goes out publicly, but also (mostly) the work that all of you are doing that is not packaged in a public way and doesn't necessarily reach hundreds or thousands of people but that you are all diligently doing every single day.

The reason we share you as an example, Dianna, is there are many listening to this who feel that they are perhaps entering what you might call a slower period of life or a different period of life. And yet

there are actually so many of you who, in your sixth, seventh, or even eighth decade on Earth, are just beginning to have energetic epiphanies and allowing yourself to be the conduit of energy that you have never before experienced or seeded on Earth. That is going to be the most important period of your life.

We say this not to denigrate all that came before, but more to remind you that until you are finished on this planet as a human being, breathing, there is plenty more to experience, to seed, and to do on Earth.

And so, Dianna, we use you as an example in that way. That is why taking as many naps as you need to adjust to the ever-changing, tumultuous frequencies on this planet is *vital*. That is why we always say self-care is not a luxury; it is a necessity. And you take care of yourself by monitoring when you need to rest, when you need to power down. You are not meant to be "on" all the time, and your human, biological bodies cannot handle spiritual frequency all day long, every day of the week. So, you do need to let yourself ebb and flow and go through the seasons. And that is true for all of you.

DIANNA:

Thank you very much for this behind-the-scenes conversation. It was a lot of fun.

THE Z'S:

Good to speak with you as ever, and good to connect with this radius of souls who are reading or listening to this information in order to multiply their own energy and ability on this planet.

Good.

In peace and in love to all.

ACKNOWLEDGMENTS

Firstly, thank you to all of you who read and enjoyed Book One! It was heartwarming to see the work go out to so many of you and be so well received.

Secondly, thank you, Dianna. What a journey we are having! I love the duality of the strength and the delicacy of this project, as well as the new element it gives to our friendship.

Thank you, Steven and Douglas, for the support and love you continue to give us both while we are making this happen; and thank you, Douglas, for the very specific energy you bring to the project.

Thank you to the wonderful members of my online Portal community, who heard these conversations first; your enthusiasm about the content encouraged and supported this publishing journey in so many ways.

Thank you, Anna Harris and Marti Bradley, for all your work with the transcriptions and initial editing; and Kristen Cashman, for your diligent editing work to bring the book across the finish line.

Trent Barfield and Tracy Cunningham, for the beautiful book design and layout; and Jake Baca, Chris Welch, and Davor Bozic, for skillfully capturing and mixing the audio recording that became the words in this book.

Thank you to my friends and contemporaries who were willing to read and endorse the book — your energy of support is felt, and I'm grateful.

Thank you, Marc Allen, Georgia Hughes, Kim Corbin, and the entire teams at both Lee Harris Energy and New World Library. Thank you *all* for your work and skill in bringing this book to life and helping us to take it out into the world. A beautiful collaboration between many great hearts, minds, and talents.

And lastly, thank you to the Z's. I don't always fully or immediately understand everything we are doing together energetically, but it always feels true and like home. Even though we now do this in more of a public and group setting, those feelings have never changed since that very first day when I privately heard you twenty-three years ago.

Here's to the unexpected journey life takes us on!

Love and light to all,
Lee Harris
December 2022

ABOUT THE AUTHORS

Lee Harris is a globally acclaimed energy intuitive, channeler, and musician who offers grounded, practical teachings focused on helping conscious, intuitive, and sensitive people heal, thrive, and live a better life. His first channeled book, *Energy Speaks*, became an instant bestseller, as did *Conversations with the Z's, Book One*. His intuitive messages and teachings reach millions each month via his free and highly popular monthly "Energy Update" videos. His monthly members' community, The Portal, offers tools and interactive live teachings to go deeper with his work and connect with a worldwide community. Lee offers over a hundred audio recordings and online courses for navigating a soul-led life with clarity, empowerment, and optimism. He also mentors creatives, healers, and entrepreneurs on how to bring their gifts and talents into the world via his free *Impact the World* podcast. His workshops, held around the globe, are adventures into the deepest aspects of living, loving, and awakening. As a musician and artist himself, Lee believes deeply in the healing power of our creativity, and his acclaimed albums, including *Timelines, I Am Peace, Transmissions,* and *Awaken* (produced by his label, Golden World Music with Davor Bozic), have ranked as high as number one on the iTunes and Amazon New Age charts. Learn more at leeharrisenergy.com.

Dianna Edwards is a psychotherapist and author dedicated to helping people discover their own authenticity through conscious awareness. She is passionate about developing and supporting ways that each of us can transform our daily experiences into opportunities for self-knowledge, empowerment, and wisdom. It is her joy to contribute her time and resources to the local communities where she lives. She is the author of the award-winning *Meet Patou* book series, written to support children and adults in understanding and processing some of life's more emotional challenges. The books have been donated to educational and health-focused institutions. To reach a wider audience, the three-book series was recently turned into free online videos on YouTube. Dianna is especially interested in opening up the topic of death and dying into a more conversant subject. Her involvement with Lee Harris in *Conversations with the Z's* arose out of her interest to assist Lee in expanding his incredible body of work as the world becomes more open and curious about the development of its greater potential. For more information about Dianna's work, visit wisdomtranscends.com.